Hands On The Wheel

Getting Control Of Your Life

SHEENA MONNIN

TABLE OF CONTENTS

FORWARD

I held the paper in my hands and cried.

I thought surely my life was over. *How could someone, anyone, want to intentionally crush me financially with such seeming malice and ill will?* I was in my twenties. I couldn't help but think that my future was completely gone. I had no hope. I had no chance.

All I had done was exercise my right of freedom of speech, relaying a personal experience. Now, I had been served papers notifying me that I was being sued for 10 million dollars. Sued by an organization owned by a man who had enough money to last him 10 lifetimes over again. A man who had called me names and demeaned me repeatedly in public. A man who did not know me, but who did surely know that a 27-year-old would not have even a quarter of a million dollars to her name, let alone multiple millions.

The extremism of it baffled me. Was I such a threat that it was determined by the opposing side to shut me down and close my mouth from speaking, no matter the cost? Was I so close to uncovering something long since hidden that it required such a response of overwhelming force? These thoughts and more went through my mind again and again.

How in the world was I expected to handle this? The mean comments, intended to blacken my reputation and paint me into something I was not. The pressure to change my words, retract my true statements and, ultimately, mold myself into an image that was not true. The millions of dollars that I did not have. The horror of seeing my face all over the media after living a very normal life under the radar of the world's attention.

To be labeled by Donald Trump, his wife Melania Trump, his daughter Ivanka Trump, and his attorney Michael Cohen, not to mention his then-President of the Miss Universe Organization, Paula Schugart, as someone who was a 'poor loser', had 'sour grapes', and just wanted her 'fifteen minutes of fame' was crushing to my spirit. I knew who I was but now the world saw me as the above people painted me with their cunning words. Only Paula Schugart could claim to even know me, as she was the one who supervised the events in Las Vegas at the 2012 Miss USA pageant.

I looked into the weeks and months ahead, keeping in mind the private threats from Trump's attorney that I would be hammered and crushed with intention from his boss, and I felt empty inside. In a way, I could hide in that emptiness. It was a shield that helped me stop feeling the violation of trust and the pain of cruel, manipulative words. Even my State Director, Randy Sanders, violated his word to me. He had repeatedly and publicly claimed that he was 'Papa Sanders' to the ladies who won titles in the states he had purchased the pageant rights to. He claimed that we could tell him anything and it would remain absolutely confidential between us. When push came to shove, he not only violated my trust, but also collaborated with the others to paint my excellent reputation as a committed titleholder and quality human being in a negative light. The emptiness of it all gnawed at me.

Maybe you, too, have felt this?

But eventually the emotions returned, multiple times, and along with the emotions, the temptation to feel hatred for many of the people who had tried to hurt me. I wanted to harm them the same way they had harmed me. I wanted to say nasty, unfounded things about them in public. And though I chose not to, there were countless times I just wanted to get even. To say I did not would be to misrepresent the humanness that is in all of us. But in the end, I can look back and see that, just as they chose their approach and their words with intention, I also chose my approach and my words with intention. I took the high road, not because it was easier, but because it was the right thing to do. It's okay to have feelings. It's not okay to allow those feelings to control you. As difficult as that philosophy is to live by, I did my best to live by it.

I don't think any of us really enjoy admitting we were bullied.

I know I don't. The truth is, *I was bullied*. The truth is, *it did hurt*. I know what it feels like to dread the next morning because you don't know what new attack is going to be waged against you. I know what it feels like to lose friends because they are afraid of the bully. I know what it feels like to lose everything, and have the entire world watching while I did.

I also know what it feels like to grip the wheel of your life so tightly that your hands almost become paralyzed in that position. I know how to dig deep and grit my teeth and say to myself a hundred times a day, 'I will NOT give in' because that is what I did. Every day. For over two years.

Each of us has the power of choice. Sometimes we don't think we do because outside factors are determined to try to control us, push us around, or bully us. I must tell you with all encouragement: you DO have the power of choice; you CAN overcome this; you WILL walk away stronger and filled with well-deserved self-respect…IF you don't allow the bullies in your life to dictate how you feel, what you do, or even what you think.

This book is written from a heart that's been there, the place where perhaps you are. Maybe our bullies look different, or maybe your controlling factors aren't people. The principle is the same. Life can become really, really difficult. We can be really, really tempted to quit or back down or step away and let the richer or more powerful people win. Or, we can stand our ground and be that small voice of truth speaking into the inflated egos around us.

As we walk through each chapter together, remember your value. Celebrate your value. And never allow anyone or anything to take that value away. I'm proud of you for taking this first step. I'm proud of you for believing that life can be different. We can make it different, one choice at a time.

THE STORM

Imagine this: A large, dark cloud is hovering over you. Lightning bolts shoot from it. Thunder rumbles ominously. Everywhere you go, the cloud goes. Everything you do, it's there, casting shadows of inky blackness around you as far as you can see. One step forward for you, one step forward for the cloud. Every step you take, it keeps pace. You search for a way out but you can't seem to outrun the cloud. You're caught in the storm. Your thoughts are racing, jumbled. The more you stay under it, the closer it pulls in around you, the stronger its force. It starts to feel like a cage. It starts to look like a cage. You're trapped. As time moves on, you become used to the cage. You forget what life was like without its confines. You forget that you deserve to walk in freedom away from the storm.

Until one day something happens…and you remember.

You see the cloud for what it is: a controlling force in your life that doesn't have any right over you except the rights you are giving it.

You identify the cage and you put a name to it. By naming it and calling it out, you take away some of its power. You start to remember your worth, your value. You speak your value. You act on your value. And then, an amazing thing happens. You see a ray of light. The all-consuming darkness of the cage weakens as you become stronger. The lightning bolts of the cloud soften, giving way to a gentle ray of sunlight, and eventually go away. The thunderous tones coming from the cloud stop telling you that you have no voice, that you have no worth, that you are defeated.

You stand stronger, and the cloud becomes mere smoke. For some of us, the cloud goes away completely. Sometimes, though, your cloud may never fully disappear. But the truth is, it doesn't have to hold power over you any more. It doesn't have to be everywhere you go, pushing you and pulling you, trying to squash you.

Because you've learned what I have learned.

~§~
People can't control me unless I allow them to.
Circumstances can't control me unless I allow them to.
~§~

It's difficult for many of us to admit to ourselves that we are allowing others to control us. The thought makes us feel uncomfortable. And maybe, we don't yet understand how unhealthy it is when we give our personal power away.

As we progress through this book, chapter-by-chapter, it is my hope that you will see how you can walk out from under the storms of life without losing your boundaries, freedom, and self-confidence. Storms will come. But not all of our storms have to leave permanent marks on our lives.

SECTION ONE

HOW DOES CONTROL LOOK IN MY LIFE?

SHEENA MONNIN

WHAT IS CONTROL?

Many of us are experiencing unhealthy control in our lives. We just may not see it yet. We may not yet understand the sometimes subtle and sometimes glaring differences between having healthy connectivity with others and allowing someone else to enter the realm of your personal power and take it away.

The truth is, having accountability is good. Being controlled by someone else is not. Having boundaries is good. Feeling obligated and worn out is not. These boundary lines will look different for each person. Keeping our personal boundaries in check is an ongoing process. Once we give a little bit of our personal rights away, it's like a landslide that gains momentum with each inch it consumes. It could be that already an area or two has surfaced in your mind where you may have given control away. Let's explore how unhealthy it is when this happens. For many, this is the first time we have thought about it, and it could be that we don't know what giving our power away even looks like or feels like.

Think about it like this, you're watching your favorite movie. You open a box of chocolates with the intention of only eating one piece while the movie is playing. But an hour later you look down and half the box is empty. How did that happen? You don't remember eating all the pieces. Your intention wasn't to eat all the pieces. Your intention was only to eat one. Why didn't you stop at one piece? You may say, 'It's because I really love chocolate, Sheena'. Fair answer. But I think for most of us there's something deeper.

The movie is your life. It's playing nonstop, 24/7. You may love your life, or you may want to change it. Regardless of how great your life is, it's still running constantly and you can't push *pause*. The chocolate is a controlling factor in your life. You see, very rarely do we give our control away carte blanche. Very rarely do we see a controlling person or situation approach us and announce to the world, 'I'm going to allow this person to control me!'

More commonly we don't recognize the potential for control. Or, if we do, we don't intend to give our control away. Like the chocolate in the box, it happens with one little move as you pick up the piece and you look at it. It seems harmless enough. Hey, you even like chocolate, remember? It's not so bad to pick up one piece. But the next thing you know as life is unfolding around you, you've moved from one piece to ten pieces. That controlling factor has gained strength as you've unwittingly given it power, one decision at a time. At the end of the day, you've stopped loving chocolate because you now associate chocolate with the negative controlling factors in your life.

I've seen this a lot in my consulting job. Our brains are wired to make associations quickly. We connect a person or an experience to an emotion, and the next thing we know, we've created a trigger. Some triggers are good. They send happy hormones racing through our minds. But most triggers that I see are negative. People feel they can't stop these triggers from going off at work or at home. The root cause is most often the control factor. At some point, the single piece of chocolate became half a box of chocolates and we feel trapped.

~§~
If you are tired of feeling trapped, you've come to the right place.
~§~

Life is not meant to be a burden. You are not meant to be locked in a cage. You are meant to have a clear mind and a full heart. You are meant to be free.

George was a nice man. He was successful, charismatic, intelligent, and he wanted to hire me to help his company. He was open to change and open to growth. He saw that his staff could benefit from leadership training. Everything seemed ready to go, and he was excited to sign on the dotted line and start the training. A funny thing happened next, though, that changed all of the positive energy he and his team were experiencing as they anticipated the benefits of the training. A week of silence went by. I never received the signed contract. I was busy with other clients and I didn't push him. When I did contact him, he hedged for about ten minutes. Eventually the truth came out. Someone very close to him had made it her priority to squash the idea of staff training. She had berated him privately, and essentially threatened him on many levels that if he hired anyone outside the company to assess the employees and conduct leadership training, she was going to make every day miserable for him. And she could. She was his wife. I realized something very acutely in that moment.

~§~
The most controlled and manipulated people often do not even see how much they are being controlled. They cannot see the situation the way others can from the outside looking in.
~§~

Why is this true? Why did George allow someone to shut down much-needed training without putting up resistance, without standing his ground on what he believed was the best thing for the company? The answer is sad for anyone in that situation. When a person has been controlled for a long period of time, it starts to feel normal. In fact, many people lose the desire to break out of a controlling situation because the thought of absolute freedom scares them.

What will I do without this person, this dark cloud, hovering over everything I do and say? Can I get back in the driver's seat and start making my own decisions again? Will they follow through on their threats? Is every negative thing they have said about me and my skills going to play out in reality?

The unknown is sometimes far more intimidating than the bossy, overbearing, manipulative people in our lives. The reason we fear responsible freedom is that we have forgotten the glorious sensations of being in control of our lives.

I've talked with countless people about how to regain control in their lives. Most people in the business world feel that they have very little opportunity or freedom to exercise control. They report to someone and they have specific tasks they are responsible for. Other people feel they have been empowered, but the word 'control' has enough negative connotations in their minds that they will not utilize this freedom.

Let's talk about this concept for a minute. Is it a bad thing to be in control? No, it's not. And, yes, it is.

Common sense tells us that it is appropriate for me to be in control of my life as long as I am *not* attempting to control you as well. No, it's not a bad thing to be in control of my life. Yes, it is a bad thing if I take my boundaries, beliefs, priorities, and agendas and push them onto you. Some people have an easier time than others walking the line between controlling themselves and their own lives versus becoming the dark cloud for someone else.

Have you ever played tug-of-war? It's a fun team-oriented game that involves a thick rope, a boundary line in the ground, and lots of muscle. People split into two teams, each team holding tightly to their end of the rope. The middle of the rope is marked and pulled taut over the boundary line that separates the teams. If Team A starts to pull harder than Team B, the middle of the rope is pulled across the boundary line and Team A will win. The opposite is also true. Occasionally, you'll encounter two teams of equal strength. If this happens, what does that mean for the middle of the rope? That's right. It stays solidly in place over the boundary line. Both teams are holding their ground without either team crossing the boundary line into the other team's territory.

Already you can see the analogy here. In your life, you may be operating solo on your end of the rope instead of on a team, but the fact is you're still holding a rope. You just may not realize it yet. Imagine any person in your life on the other end of the rope. You're both pulling because human nature dictates that each person, at some level, will always try to get their own way. If you take a break from holding onto the rope to eat a piece of chocolate, what happens? The rope slides across the boundary line a little. When that happens it's tough to get your personal power back.

What if the person on the other side starts taunting you? For some, that may incite you to pull harder and try to win more. For others, it crushes you a little and you let go just enough to lose more of your personal power. Is it bad that you are trying to hold on to your end of the rope? Is it bad that you are trying to keep the boundary line in place? No, of course it's not bad. You know what it is, though? It's you trying to control your life. You're not stealing others' control of their lives, but you are standing your own ground. This is balance, this is appropriate, and this is being respectful of yourself and of others.

Often when people see control in terms of boundaries and fairness, the concept of being in control doesn't seem too far-fetched. It seems normal and natural. It seems healthy.

At this point it's important to stop so you can do a little self-assessing. It's amazing to me how many of us go through life without ever exploring our thoughts and feelings. A large part of staying in control is understanding what builds you up and what tears you down. If you're on Team A from our earlier scenario and you hear a teammate start complaining, how does that influence you? If you hear that same person muttering how impossible the situation is or how much better the other team is, does that trigger a change in your own attitude in certain ways? How about this, you're elected team captain but the people standing on the sidelines start cheering for their personal favorite on your team…and it's not you. Does that affect your sense of self-worth?

Take a moment and ponder these points. The more you understand yourself, the easier it will be to monitor where the boundary line of the rope is, and why you may have started giving control away.

- What motivates me to try harder, perform more consistently, and continue my forward momentum?
- What changes could happen that would derail the above?
- What would I need to do to get my personal power back? Am I willing to stay watchful each day and monitor my levels of control?
- What benefits would come from self-monitoring?

The next time you are called upon by life's circumstances to stand up for yourself and maintain control in a situation, remember the game tug-of-war. The visual of where the boundary line is can be helpful when it comes to assessing whether or not you are giving control away or starting to control others too much.

WHY DO WE NEED TO MAINTAIN CONTROL?

Routinely I arrive early to appointments, especially with new clients. This allows me time to watch the interactions between the employees and begin my assessment even before the training starts. One day, upon arriving at a training session with the company owner, I was escorted into the conference room. The door was left open. A few minutes later, an employee walked into the room. He was slightly frenetic, thinking he was late for a team training session. My training. The only problem was, I hadn't been scheduled to give a group training that day. The man rushed over and shook my hand and offered an apology about being late. He had taken the day off but received a message that a non-optional training session was being held that morning. He had come in ready to learn, which was impressive to me. I checked my calendar and could not find the training he was referring to. He quickly, and understandably, became annoyed at the person who had sent the message to him. We had to explore what went wrong and eventually reached the bottom of the problem.

Long story short, this man had come in early on his day off because the person scheduling the training had made an error. The reason for the error? Jet lag from recent travel and confusion over which contract with my company had been approved by the boss, my client. Valid to a point, but still not the full picture.

When I dug a little deeper I saw two problems, both related to control being given away and excuses being made. First, the man who rushed in when the training notice message was sent, gave control of the situation away the moment he failed to verify the message source and question the last minute oddity of a mandatory training session. Going even deeper, we saw this need to please as an unhealthy theme in his life. He was allowing his desire to be excellent to morph into the belief that if he ever stopped pleasing others, his value would disappear. Thoughts of annoyance and loss of self were occurring, clouding his rational logic. This is called psychological clutter.

~§~
Psychological clutter is comprised of the issues we face each day but don't process, deal with, and then move on from them.
~§~

Instead, they sit in our subconscious causing us stress, doubt, and aggression. We'll return to this concept in a moment.

The second problem I discovered through a series of conversations and direct questions was with the person doing the scheduling. They had gone on autopilot and were not paying attention to details—details that affect the lives of others. Have you ever been so comfortable with your job that you feel you can go on autopilot? Now, I admit there are times when autopilot is beneficial and produces good results, like when I'm driving my car I don't want to have to think about every maneuver needed to get me from point A to point B. But when you're an employee and you go on autopilot, things are a little different. Mistakes are made that waste company time and money.

There are many reasons for an employee going on autopilot. Many have been performing at the same level in their job for years without much improvement. They are tolerably productive and the quality of their work is consistent. In short, they're comfortable. They're either not in a position to get a promotion or they don't want to change where they are. When someone like me comes in and starts encouraging a game plan that would shake up their routine, I'm usually labeled as the bad guy. But the truth is, if an employee is so complacent that autopilot occurs every day, that's not beneficial for the overall health of the company.

The worst part of autopilot is we turn off our emotions and often our empathy. We lose the connection to what we are doing. The better-performing employees maintain a level of connectivity to their tasks. They take ownership of what they are doing. When I see an employee take ownership and pride in their productivity, I quietly applaud them. Why? *Because they have chosen not to give control of their own performance away to routine. They have kept their priorities clear, and as a result fewer mistakes are made.*

Priorities are a daily fact of the adult life. Developing and keeping priorities is directly linked to the concept of psychological clutter. If you're like most of us, you have probably had a bad day. When you think about those bad days, does your mind process information differently than on a good day? Naturally, it does. On bad days, one of the main differences in the way information is received, perceived, and funneled into action has to do with clarity.

Clarity is lost when we have accumulated mental baggage in our minds that we have not dealt with. Either we don't know it is there or we just don't want to process it. This loss of clarity shows up in a variety of forms. Sometimes it's the loss of a clear purpose or mission for your life. Other times, it's more miniscule and hard to identify. It seems as if you have no ability to retain information the way you used to, or you find you zone out mentally more than you'd like.

When people share with me that they are having a hard time focusing at work, that their brain feels preoccupied while also feeling vacant, that they go home and check out mentally for hours in front of the TV, I usually know what's going on. It could be that they are in an organizational position that is inherently stressful and their one segment of the day that is 'me time' is to zone out and allow the telomeres in their brain the chance to stop over-firing. More frequently than a stressful job, however, loss of clarity is due to unresolved issues, unchallenged negative self-images, unspoken fears, or guilt from the past. In short, psychological clutter is controlling their minds and hindering them from the passionate, organized, and successful life that they want. It feels like a bad day over and over again with no end in sight. It feels like your psychological vision is blurry and no matter how frequently you blink, things never quite shift into focus and stay there.

How do you know if you've given ground over to psychological clutter? Countless avenues to this dead end exist. Here are the three most common I've encountered:

Outdated, old, or incomplete To-Do lists

Why is this important to handle? If a list is a month old, why should you care if the items are crossed off or not? The reason is simple. Your brain remembers what has been finished and what has not. Even if you can't pull the details to the forefront of your mind, the imprint of the list is floating around in your subconscious. If this situation isn't addressed, many people experience anxiety that they can't pinpoint the source of, fear of failure that seems to have little to no foundation, and a sense of neediness tied to being overwhelmed without a distinct explanation of what is so overwhelming in life. Often, just by searching out those lists, taking a pen, and crossing off the items that are irrelevant or already completed gives people a lot of psychological space and the sense of mental freedom. Combine the remaining undone items into one list and stay on it until it's finished. You'll be amazed at the difference that form of accomplishment can bring.

Unresolved arguments, disagreements, and lies

Have you ever heard the statement, 'There's an elephant in the room'? That phrase means there's something huge and negative that remains unspoken and needs to be handled. *Everyone* knows the issue is there, but no one is willing to discuss it. Generally, it is an issue that makes people uncomfortable, and the more time that passes the more obvious the unspoken issue becomes. The use of 'elephant' in that statement is to show how something so huge and obvious can be pushed to the side by the act of our will. I have seen elephants up close and in person. They are hard to miss. But if we put effort into it, we could ignore one elephant if we needed to.

Imagine for a moment an entire herd of elephants, and how much space they are taking up as a group. Imagine that the group is gathering in your mind. Each new argument you haven't resolved, each disagreement where you feel you were treated unfairly but never could clear the air, and each lie you have told in order to make yourself look good or get out of hot water is another elephant being added to your mind. By the age of 35, that's a lot of elephants. By 55, the amount of clutter that has accumulated is staggering.

But the silent, unspoken herd of elephants occupying your brain is exactly what unresolved people issues start to feel like over time. Eventually, others notice the herd, maybe not the specifics, but the presence of those unresolved issues is more than a little apparent. It causes undue defensiveness, workaholism, fidgeting, inappropriately timed humor, awkwardness, and increasingly high levels of anxiety.

Let's face it, we are human. We've all accumulated elephants. Take some time right now to get rid of the herd by confronting the elephants that have accumulated and make it a practice each day to keep that space under control. This may involve reaching out to people and clearing the air between you and them. Or it could mean letting go of an offense that someone caused against you but never apologized for. Whatever your elephant is, find the source and handle the issue until it is resolved

Expectations you have failed to live up to

This clutter is frankly more difficult to eradicate than the other two mentioned above. Living a life that is wrought with expectations can be damaging, especially if the expectations for yourself are not your own. For the high performers, living with your own self-expectations is hard enough, but add on top of that those of others, and before you know it, you've given your personal power away by chasing what is important to them rather than what is important to you.

Often, I find the expectations of parents, role models from childhood, and early bosses have the most impact on how people perceive and measure their success. These expectations turn into mountains of pressure constantly pushing down upon your mind. These mountains directly influence your self-image. Your self-talk is colored and shaded by the voices of early influencers in your life. Be very aware of how the expectations of others have shaped your ideas of success, happiness, love, and priorities. Choose to replace the thoughts of failure and shame with thoughts that are true. Each time an old, damaging thought comes in, get it out immediately. This version of psychological clutter can be beaten, but it will take a lot of work for you to ultimately reprogram your mind and break free of this type of control.

If you have a minute now, take a little time and think through other preoccupations and forms of clutter you have gathered in your mind.

We all are either digging in deeper where we are, moving forward, or dragging the past along with us, partly still living there. People tell me occasionally that sometimes they just want to take a break from self-development. Life is moving fast and they just want to rest upon the lessons learned up to that point. They think that taking a break means that no ground will be lost. The opposite is true. This is why I give small tasks to initiate small changes. If someone feels dumped on with a myriad of changes to make, they will often dig in deeper and justify why it's better to remain where they are. But if they feel accomplishment each day by finishing small things, they can start to break free from controlling factors and live victoriously over all the elephants, chocolate, and yards of rope that have been controlling them for years. Remember, life is not stagnant. You are not stagnant. Life is a constant exchange of energy. Your life does not come with a pause button.

If you decrease your psychological clutter you will find you don't need as much autopilot or zoning out time. You will discover that your brain feels free and your mood lighter. Your perspective of your life and the people and opportunities in your life will change for the better. You'll see more tasks being completed and less time being wasted. Your sense of value will improve.

To me, all of this is worth working for.

SHEENA MONNIN

THE VICTIMHOOD MYTH

Sometimes bad things happen in life and *it's not your fault*. You may have been lied to, manipulated, mislead, or taken advantage of. Other times when bad things pop up in life, it is actually your fault. You may have failed to plan properly, made a very unwise choice, or cut a corner. Theoretically, it should be easy to identify when we are a victim of an injustice or wrongdoing and when we are not. There are enough mystery novels that involve theft, corruption, and crime for us to see examples of people who are victims. We may not have had something stolen from us or been the target of a violent crime, but we may be a victim in smaller ways. Chances are right now, off the top of your head, you could probably tell me half a dozen instances where you were taken advantage of in some way and were a victim to someone else's selfish behavior. Chances are, also, that you could probably pull to the front of your mind instances where you stretched the truth a little to make it seem like you were an innocent victim when in reality you just wanted to get a free pass or make someone else look worse than they were.

The question is, when we are not a legitimate victim, why do we still at times act like one? Why do we point fingers and willingly accept sympathy and support from others when we don't actually deserve it, when it's not healthy for us? If we're honest, we all have done this at one time or another in our lives.

There was an online video that was floating around social media for months. The footage was adorable and demonstrates how young we are when we first test out the possibility of getting off the hook by blaming someone else who is actually innocent. The video was of a little girl who was in trouble because she had used fingernail polish to paint her doll's fingernails and then started painting the carpet as well. The video opens with the girl looking repentant and doing her best to let her dad know how bad she felt that she had painted the carpet. Her dad asked her why she did it and the entire expression on her young face changed. An idea had been born in her mind. She proceeded to claim that it was her doll's idea that she painted the carpet. She went with this for a little while until her dad questioned the notion of her doll having an idea. Then the little girl claimed that not only was her doll the originator of the idea that using fingernail polish in the bedroom was a good idea, but the doll had actually insisted she use the fingernail polish and paint all the nails of all the dolls. With her dad's promptings she eventually admitted to some of the fault and promised to never do it again.

One of the reasons this cute video was so popular was because we all can relate to the child's reasoning and thought process. She saw a way out of a difficult situation (and having to sit in 'time out') by pushing the blame on someone else. If her doll had indeed been the one to make her paint the carpet, then the little girl was a victim and not liable to correction. In reality, we all know who was responsible in this example. We can watch the video and chuckle at the child's quick wit and cleverness. It stops being adorable, though, when we do this as adults.

For some people, the tendency to shift blame is a strong driving force within them. At its core, though, we are looking for control when we take on the role of a false victim. But it's not the healthy kind of control that we've been talking about, the type where you stay on your side of the tug of war boundary line. Blame shifting is attempting to control others, moving into a realm that is not healthy.

I'm not entirely certain of the reason, but it seems that our culture is breeding the mentality of victimhood. Instead of taking ownership, people today are encouraged to find a reason (or an excuse) why they failed or why they fell short of the mark. The idea that 'everyone wins' or everyone receives a trophy even if they didn't actively participate or win breeds the mentality of expectancy.

It looks like this: If I lose it's not my fault; it's the coach's fault or the guy next to me is to blame. If I didn't practice it's also not my fault; my parents didn't make me practice so it's their fault. Either way, trying or sitting out, I'll still get a trophy and be rewarded.

I'm not saying we all should strive to be emotionless robots taking the blame for everything that goes wrong in life. Not at all. But I do think that our first response shouldn't be an excuse. My psychology degree taught me the importance of processing our thoughts and our feelings (remember our previous chapter on getting rid of psychological clutter). But I also know how quickly channels can be formed in our brains. If we play the victim once and are rewarded for it, how likely are we to try it again when we're in a pinch? Quite likely. The more the channel is reinforced, the easier it will be to access it. Before we know it, we've built a highway in our mental processing that tells us not only is it okay to be a victim, but it's the best way to navigate through life. In reality, is it the best way? Let's explore this.

If you're a passenger in a car and someone runs a red light, hitting the car you're in, are you the victim? Of course you are! For one thing, you weren't driving. For another, the car you were riding in was legally passing through an intersection. The person running the red light clearly violated your expectation to travel safely. By hitting your car and injuring you, not only were your rights violated, you were violated. Clearly, you are a legitimate victim.

Not all scenarios are this cut and dry. A friend of mine was a member of a service organization. After several years of volunteer and organizational service, she put her name forward and was accepted to be on the Board of Directors. A few more years went by and eventually she decided that she would like to be the President of the organization. She was beyond excited at the prospect. Why was she so excited? Years of sitting on the sidelines had allowed her to see with objectivity the weaknesses of the organization. She had formed a solid plan of improvement. But, there was a problem. Several key members of the board and long-standing advisors had been in their positions for over a decade and were resistant to the changes she wanted to make. But my friend is persistent and smart. She tried to keep the changes small and she worked hard to present her ideas in the most well-researched and logical way.

A solid year went by before, over lunch, I heard her tale about the overt obstinacy of the board members and their opposition to her. By then, it had turned into a concentrated effort to undermine not only her efforts, but also her credibility. More than angering her, it really affected her feelings. After all, she loved the organization and the message of service they stood for.

I listened to her story for over an hour. Each detail revealed to me the degree of betrayal she felt. While being overtly sympathetic is not my initial reaction most of the time, I did sincerely feel for her. That is, I did until our food arrived and I had time to think through her experience with my logical brain instead of my emotions. The truth is, deep down she felt like an innocent victim. And let's face it, being in her shoes and being undermined by people you once trusted and respected is never a good feeling. But here's what I posited to her as I gave her feedback about her experience and discussed how to regain control of a situation that had morphed into something monstrous.

First, I suggested that she was not a victim because she admitted to knowing how challenging it would be to initiate change in an organization that was so committed to tradition and honoring the way past leaders had guided the group. She was not caught off guard. She saw it coming. Secondly, I pointed out that in the beginning the opposition had been manageable. Somewhere along the path both sides stopped communicating. I asked her what would have happened if at that juncture she would have slowed down the changes and actually invested time communicating with those who were grumbling. 'It's hard to know' was her answer. And she was right. Projecting possible outcomes is not always easy. But my point to her was that she unknowingly gave control of the situation away by losing touch with those who had traditionally held a lot of power over the members. She mistook their silence for a begrudging acceptance of the changes she wanted. I explained that a victim is one who, for one reason or another, cannot get control of a situation. She saw my point and we moved on.

My friend could have stood like a brick wall and refused to allow the negative energy coming at her to influence her thinking and reactions, but often when we are in the middle of a tumultuous situation we are unable to think clearly. We are tempted to run with our emotions and start to point fingers and shift blame. We cry out for all to hear or we act out for all to see: I am the victim!

Is there someone in your life who is stronger than you are? Someone who has more influence and more power? If they are using that power well, then you may not be tempted to pull out the victim card. As we've seen above, there are true victims of circumstances. But there are also those who mistakenly believe they are a victim, when in reality, they are not.

Can we be honest right now? Think about a recent example, a recent time, when your initial reaction was to point fingers at someone else and blame them for something that happened to you that you didn't like?

I'll share a mistake I made where I took on the victim mentality without good reason to. I was working on finalizing a contract for a company. I sent over the changes they requested. Four days went by and the training was scheduled to start within a week. My contact person was generally very prompt and, I confess, I became a little impatient. However, it is my policy to not harass people. Sometimes processing paperwork takes longer than one anticipates. A weekend passed and Monday came around. That morning I said something to this effect to myself, 'Why can't people just be professional? Why does this *always* happen to me?' You guessed it, I had just slid over into playing the role of a victim.

I sat down to write a reminder email to my contact person. The email address wasn't coming up automatically so I scrolled through my inbox looking for a prior email communication thread. Lo and behold, sitting there in my inbox was the contract *sent the previous week*, waiting for me to sign. Somehow I had overlooked it. I felt completely embarrassed that I had been thinking grumbling thoughts and feeling rejected by the company. All thoughts of how perfectly professional I was compared to everyone else were shattered and reality set in. To drive the point home even more, as I sat there processing my victimhood thoughts in order to get rid of them, a follow up email came in to me from the company asking why they hadn't heard a confirmation of my receipt of the contract! Feeling a little sheepish I hastened to respond and soon we were back on track with the timing of things.

When we start seeing ourselves as a victim we are prone to exaggerate things. We tend to generalize behaviors and see ourselves as more perfect than we are while everyone else is making mistakes or being irresponsible. I started to do this as well. For one thing, most people are professional. For another, whenever we use the words 'always' or 'never' in our self-talk it's usually a sign of victimhood.

It's true, we *all* can pull out the victim card and begin to feel sorry for ourselves. How can we recognize when this is happening? We can't recognize this if we aren't self-aware.

~§~
Being self-aware is one of the more challenging parts of most of our journeys toward regaining control of our lives.
~§~

In true self-awareness we need to be honest, no matter what we see through our time of reflection. Each day we must be cognizant of our thoughts, our reactions, the way we see people and the way we interpret what they say. We must monitor our motives and what desires we have for each part of our lives. People who are not self-aware generally aren't adept at connecting with others. They are too busy being busy, acting self-important, talking in such a way to dominate the conversation, and often being passive aggressive. None of these descriptions are attractive personally or professionally. But any one of us can fall into those patterns either directly choosing that path or by feeling pushed by others who aren't self-aware.

The trick to becoming truly self-aware is to be willing to see your own filter for what it is. When we take information into our minds it goes through several filters, letting us know if we are safe, happy, upset, or indifferent to the information. If our filter is dingy from years of neglect, we may need an objective outside opinion to help us see the truth of our situation. It takes time to reset our filter. If you're in a stressful or fast-paced job, the effort of keeping your filter balanced and objective will be greater than it is for those who have fewer responsibilities and more time to process interactions as they occur.

This leads me to the observation that most happy people are those who have taken the time to recall events of the day and deal with them in their minds. If you have failed to complete a task or finish an accomplishment and feel badly about it, don't think that sleeping on the problem or disappointment will fix it. Instead, not dealing with it will create more clutter in our minds, and we already know what that can do to us. If you argued with someone, you may need a day or two to get over your emotions. But in the meantime, it's vital that you go over the events in your mind and strive to move through the event processing at a good pace. Otherwise, who knows, you may just find an excuse to pull out your victim card and wave it around like a banner.

Putting the banner of victimhood away after carrying it for years or decades is not as hard as you may think. As with most issues, it really does go back to how much we want to maintain healthy control of our lives. Take a look at the signs of victimhood below. Be patient with yourself if you identify with several of them. We all start somewhere. Believe that the path toward personal empowerment and personal control leads to benefits beyond what you can see, and don't give up. Also, you may recognize these traits in the lives of people you know and are close to. Just as you wouldn't want someone trying to change you and infringe on your personal control, tread very lightly when recognizing flaws in others and feeling the urge to correct them. Often just focusing on ourselves is a full time job and leaves little time for pointing fingers.

A victim is/will say/do:

- Not my fault
- Rarely dependable; being a victim inherently means carrying a lot of obligation to others and baggage; as such it's difficult to be reliable
- Usually defensive; can show up as passive aggressive or merely aggressive
- Often responds with denial, not understanding: 'I never said/did that.' or 'That's not what I meant' or 'You missed that deadline last week, so why are you mad that I'm a little late?'
- Rationalizes or justifies frequently

- Turns words around to make you feel like you are at fault: 'Why are you using that tone with me? Don't you know I'm just doing my best?' or 'Don't you care about my situation – you have no idea what I'm going through.' or 'You are so judgmental. I think you need help.'
- Does not want to hear your perspective
- Interrupts and interjects frequently

If a few light bulbs are going off in your mind after reading this list, that's a good thing. Remember, self-awareness is vital to regaining control of your life. I don't think it's always enough to see a behavior and label it. Labeling something can be confining and limit the accuracy of what you are labeling if you don't leave room for change and growth to occur.

~§~
Lasting change happens when we discover our motive behind the behavior.
~§~

It could be that we aren't the ones playing the role of a victim. We may know people who act in ways outlined above. For many people, playing the victim is an intentional ploy to control and manipulate others. If we make ourselves out to be helpless or hurt when we actually aren't, then it's likely that we are attempting to gain sympathy, attention, and specific words or actions from others. We know that unhealthy control is behind the behaviors when those who are acting victimized get an attitude when we don't respond to them the way they had planned, or expected. If we see such an attitude, we can be fairly certain the person is holding that banner of victimhood. If we give them what they want out of a sense of obligation or because we want to avoid the attitude, we are enabling them. And enabling others in an unhealthy behavior is a slippery slope.

When you choose to break out of the cycle of enabling a victim, a backlash of anger or manipulation or threats will likely occur. Before you decide to alter your behavior and not enable someone, be sure you are committed to seeing it through. Understand that you can't change them, but you can put your hands back on the wheel of your life and change directions in ways that are healthy for you. Don't be afraid to grow, even if those you are close to are choosing to remain in the victimhood bondage. You don't have to. You can objectively, strongly, and with certainty charge toward your own health without being held back or held responsible for others in your life who are determined to remain in an unhealthy state.

You may have to endure a lot of negativity coming at you, but if you want freedom from the cloud we discussed in the beginning of this book, you can have it. Freedom often comes with a price. But I've found in my life, the price is worth it and the reward of breaking free from whatever bondage is holding you is sweet indeed.

E + R = O

Several years ago there was a clever commercial with the tagline that asked what was in a person's wallet. The premise was that certain credit cards held more power and advantage than others. Viewers of the commercial were repeatedly challenged to examine what was in their wallet and the subconscious message of the images shown was that if you didn't have that particular credit card, you were missing out on the power to buy what you wanted when you wanted. You were lacking freedom.

I'm not prone to watching much TV, but that particular commercial has stayed with me over the years. I think the reason is the universal applicability of the message. How frequently do we check to see where our power is coming from? How often do we compare ourselves, our stuff, or our lives with others? And, how frequently do we seem to come up short?

For me, I can always tell when I'm comparing myself with someone else. Instantly my energy levels die. I concentrate all my energy on analyzing why I'm not as good as someone else, and as a result, I withdraw from people. This can last a minute, an hour, or an entire afternoon. What's interesting, though, is that when I'm happy with my job and I'm not feeling behind, it's very rare that I compare myself with others. Usually, it's on the days when I have too much mental space because work is slow or when I am experiencing a disappointment that my impulse is to compare.

If we are struggling to find peace in difficulty or purpose in the moment, why do we allow ourselves to fall into the trap of comparison?

The reasons are endless. You can take five minutes and quickly dissect what your specific triggers are in this area. Most of the time we compare out of habit, and some people receive an unhealthy sense of comfort or motivation from the routine of comparison.

~§~
Comparison is another version of us giving control away, and, when we take our control back into our own hands we give ourselves power.
~§~

Going back to the commercial, the message was strong because the wallet signified you and your power source. When you filled your wallet with the correct things, your perspective on your life improved. When your perspective improves then there is very little need or desire to compare yourself to others.

The old question, 'Is the glass half full or half empty?' rings a bell for many of us, and the answer to that question is purely based on one's perspective. Technically, both options hold merit. Whatever our perspective is, it's correct to us, it's reasonable to us, and it's obvious to us because it is built on the foundation of our thoughts, our priorities, our experiences, and our expectations.

How vital is it that we are in control of our perspective? As vital as the air we breathe, the water we drink, and the food we eat. Our perspective holds tremendous power. Often our actions will indicate our perspective. We may think that our actions are the main way our viewpoint is revealed. That is not entirely true. Our reactions also reveal what our perspective is. Our reactions show those around us what our character is, what we place value on, and how we really see a person or a difficulty. I've found our actions can be more easily controlled than our reactions. This could be true because our actions indicate that we are initiating something. We have more control when we initiate. If someone else is initiating something that elicits a negative feeling or thought from us, it's more likely that our reactions can become inflamed and, in essence, control us.

Jack Canfield made famous this equation: E + R = O.

'E' is the event. 'R' is the response. And 'O' is the outcome. Looking back at our discussion of victimization, it's easy to jump from 'E' to 'O' without considering the 'R'. If I equate the events in my life with the outcome and fail to consider how my response directly influenced the outcome, I am on the fast track to losing control of my life.

As we go through life and make decisions, keep in mind how vital our response is to situations. Did you know we could also have positive or negative responses to our own thoughts and feelings? Our thoughts very frequently are a guiding light for us.

~§~
If we follow the train of our thoughts without challenging the unhealthy ones, we are giving control away.
~§~

I've moved from house to house, and state to state quite a bit in my life. Each time I moved to a new state or house, I had the sense of starting over, especially when I was too young to be involved in packing, loading, unpacking, and arranging things in the new house. Everything was fresh and new. I'm not saying that I always wanted to move or enjoyed the process of saying goodbye to old friends, but what I can look back and see is the benefit of leaving the past behind me and moving on to new surroundings, new friends, and new routines.

I clearly remember how the older I was when I moved, the greater my sense that things were temporarily out of control became. If you've ever moved to a new place, you know the vast number of details that are involved in moving. The older I became, the more I took responsibility for my own possessions and the more I helped in the process. While I could control what I kept and what I did not keep, what I packed into the moving van and what I took with me, I could not control everything. As a child and teenager I could not control where we moved or how frequently, or, what moving service we used, or who would be our new neighbors.

~§~
Frequently there is tension in life between what can be controlled and what cannot be controlled. Wisdom is developed through handling what we can control and working with what we cannot control.
~§~

As we move through the topics in this book, I don't want you to feel that I advocate you becoming what is known as a 'control freak', the person who has to have everything nailed down without room for variables. Remember tug-of-war. That's the type of control and boundaries that we are discussing.

Take a little time today to reflect on what areas in life are appropriate for you to control and what areas are not. Like me when my family relocated, you may need to make a huge life change that you were not planning to make or desiring to make. Rather than the futile attempt to stop the life change, do what I learned to do: take responsibility where you can and keep the areas in your life you can influence under control and with proper boundaries.

If you've ever been skydiving you know how fast that initial free-fall is. For a split-second as solid ground zooms ever closer, many people feel they are going to die. Everything seems out of focus and your heart is in your throat. Even though in that moment of free-fall nothing seems under control, there is something that you can do to immediately get the situation under control. You can pull the cord and release the parachute.

Each situation comes with its own parachute: your thoughts, your perspective, and your reactions. Remember the equation E + R = O? If you take out the 'R' in the skydiving scenario, what do you get? A human pancake on the ground. It's your response of pulling the cord to release the parachute that allows you to change the outcome. You can't climb back into the plane or stop the event, but you can slow things down and find your way to the ground safely.

If you realize that *every situation* comes with a built in opportunity to *maintain control* or *release control*, you may just start to look at things differently.

What happens, though, if we give up control? What happens if we eat that one piece of chocolate or let go of that tug-of-war rope for just one minute? We give ground away to external forces. When we do this we feel negativity creep into our lives. We suffer and those around us that we care about suffer.

~§~
When we give control away we invite negative factors into our lives.
~§~

Signs of negativity include:

- Stress
- Feeling behind in projects, bills, obligations, tasks
- Falling into people pleasing instead of maintaining boundaries
- Feeling that others are out to get you, that no one can be trusted
- Thinking that you need to defend your viewpoint
- Lethargy or hyperactivity
- Depression
- Bullying tendencies
- Cynicism

Basically, the negativity that spews from us at times through our words, actions, and reactions can generally be traced to a point in our lives where we gave away a piece of control that was very near and dear to us. Since we never stopped to process it or regain that control, it has stayed on the backburner, reminding us through these negative items listed above that it is still there, and that it has power over us.

Conquer the areas you've given control away in to find the path back to peace, strength, and focus. If you want to hold onto the appropriate power over your own life, remember to control your response to the events that occur.

WHAT WOULD LIFE BE LIKE IF WE DIDN'T GIVE AWAY OUR CONTROL?

What does your perfect life look like? What is in your perfect life that is not in your life now?

When I picture my perfect life, the surroundings I want to live in, the objects I want to own, the things I want to do, the path I see toward accomplishing those things is not one of chance. It is one of intention.

I can't remember the last time I heard a successful person say something like, 'This financial milestone just happened to me; it was by chance that I met these sales goals.' Successful people don't give credit to chance. Your idea of success may be different from mine, but we both probably realize that if you want something to happen, you will need to put effort into it.

Imagine going to school to be a chiropractor and upon graduation, completion of your internship, and acquisition of your license to practice you sat in your brand new office space and waited for people to walk in, needing your services. That doesn't sound like the path toward success! What would you need to do if you wanted to see your education pay off? You would need to actively seek ways to put your knowledge into practice. This may include advertising, collaborating with established professionals in the field, and any number of ways to practice what you've studied.

It's the same for you.

You have garnered a lot of knowledge up to this point just by reading this book. The question for you to ponder and decide is what you will do moving forward. You can sit on the information and let it ruminate in your mind without taking action, or you can begin to apply it, bit by bit, until you reach a new comfort level with healthy boundaries and appropriately applied levels of control in your life. Let's face it, though. Each of us is motivated a little bit differently. I'm more motivated to change when I think of all the negative consequences I will avoid by making a positive change in my life.

If, for example, I'm told that mowing my lawn each week will ensure that I don't get a fine from my neighborhood association, I'm going to get out and mow my lawn. Or if my dentist tells me to avoid sugary drinks or else my teeth will suffer, I'm going to avoid sugary drinks.

But maybe you aren't motivated by thinking of future consequences and trying to prevent them. Maybe you are motivated by thinking of all the positive ways change will influence your life.

If I told you that mowing your lawn each week will make your grass greener and your home more attractive, it may incite you to action more than it would me. Or if your dentist told you that your teeth would look their best if you drank sugar-free drinks, you may feel that the goal is not only doable, but it's worth putting effort into.

Knowing how you are propelled into action is important. Also knowing how others are motivated is beneficial when it comes to boundaries and using a clean mental filter. If you and I were working together and I'm motivated by avoiding negatives while you're motivated by focusing on positive rewards, it's likely that my manner of expressing myself will include all the ways we can stay out of harm's way. You may perceive me as a negative person because I am so focused on what could go wrong and how to avoid it. I may be annoyed with you because all I hear is that you see silver linings in every cloud and you don't seem to want to be realistic about our possible issues. Recognizing that people are not all the same is helpful when it comes to knowing if you are off balance in your quest to get control of your life.

~§~

Every day the opportunity for annoyance will happen.
People think differently. Start now to keep your boundaries
in place while respecting the boundaries of others.

~§~

Since I know that not everyone thinks the way that I do, let's take a moment and look at all the ways staying in control will benefit your life. There are endless positive outcomes available to you when you make the changes necessary to control your life. It's exciting to consider.

The example above about our potentially differing perspectives and ways of being motivated is very common. When I'm leading a team through conflict resolution, I have noticed it's often the small things that cause teams to fracture. By the time the team leadership realizes that help is necessary, the small annoyances have morphed into something heated and damaging to the success of the enterprise. When the difficulties are examined and broken down into their foundational elements, people are amazed - and sometimes shocked - by how the seemingly huge differences of opinion started with something as small as a differing thought or perspective.

When you meet someone, you automatically assess them. Without trying to, we put people in categories in our minds. Once categorized, it's more rare than common that we can think of them in a different category. By doing this, you are subconsciously setting yourself up for either success or failure with this person in the future based on your initial presupposition. And the interesting part to consider is: you don't usually know you are doing this.

A few years ago I was working with a woman I did not care for very much. I felt she was unduly bossy and domineering. Every time I said 'yes' she seemed determined to find all the ways to say 'no'. Sound familiar? We all know people like that. I initially avoided interactions with her as much as I could in order to keep my own mental peace and calmness. Eventually it became clear this approach was not the healthiest one. Every time she contradicted me or tried to change my decision or viewpoint, I felt defensive. I don't know about you, but I don't like the way it feels to always be on guard and always feel the need to defend your ground. My preference is to try to see where the other person is coming from and meet them halfway so both myself and that person avoid unnecessary conflict (if you are a positive-outcome motivated person then you may resonate more strongly with this view: you want to meet someone halfway so you and that person can build a stronger bridge of communication and experience higher levels of satisfaction in the working relationship). I did start to see patterns with what made her satisfied with my ideas and my plans. I began to word my emails and my communication with her differently, in ways that I thought she would be able to process most efficiently. I did not let go of my tug-of-war rope, but I intentionally showed her respect in ways that she very quickly let me know she appreciated. Our interactions became productive and more efficient. And, though this is not always the case, we also built a professional friendship. I can't say that she speaks my language of respect the way that I speak hers, but the truth is: it doesn't matter. I can't control her but by controlling myself, I can make the entire situation better for all people involved.

As you go through life you will wish you could control people or at the very least influence them. But that's not reality. Instead, by maintaining your personal power in healthy ways you can experience one of the primary benefits of staying in control of your life, building a mutually respectful environment with those you interact with. Contrast that with an environment of complaining, belittling, and working against each other and you can see why a respectful environment is important for a person's overall well being.

Do you know what I did initially with the woman in the example? I inadvertently allowed her to control my thoughts and my feelings. Every time I saw an email from her I would bristle a little and grumble in my mind. That was even before I read the email. Frequently we give control away without thinking twice about it. As you move forward with the idea of keeping control, it will be easier to practice the concept with new people you meet. With people you've known for a long time you will have to work harder to create new rules of interaction with that person. It can be done, and one reward of doing so has already been revealed.

Another benefit is a marked reduction in your stress levels. If you want to feel burdens lifted from your shoulders and your sense of obligation to others decrease, by simply getting your life under control and putting yourself back in the driver's seat, you can accomplish healthy levels of personal freedom and empowerment.

It's time to revisit the topic of self-talk. A great quantity of the stress we put on ourselves is related to people. Another huge chunk of it comes from how we talk to ourselves. If we miss a gym day once this week and two gym days the following week, how objective are we in the way we talk to ourselves about the decision we made to *not* go to the gym? By negative self-talk we are creating stress and we are ultimately giving control of balanced thinking away with every emotional or untrue or exaggerated thought we allow in our minds. In this way, we can come up with endless reasons to stay away from the gym. But deep down, we will be in conflict. We know we should be going to the gym and we know we cannot truly justify not going.

The result of this internal battle fueled by negative self-talk is stress.

Each of us has our own list of things in life that bring us stress. Some of these factors are non-negotiable. No matter how balanced our thinking is, these things will still be stressful tomorrow and the next day. Huge difficulties like an illness, or a loss of someone you love, or a relationship ending, or being in the middle of a lawsuit are real stressors. And they don't disappear just by reexamining our thoughts. We can still get in control of our thoughts and reduce the impact these stressors have on us each minute of the day, but we can't label these stressors as something we are giving unnecessary space to in our lives. They will remain in our lives until they are resolved.

What about the medium sized stressors? Things like a difficult work assignment or a difficult marriage or child or sibling or parent or coworker? These things are more manageable. We can't necessarily change them but we can manage them through controlling our thoughts, reactions, and interactions.

Generally when discussing examples of stress, one or two specific stressors pop into people's minds. What stresses you out? Whatever came to your mind, examine how much the stressor is influencing your daily thoughts, your self-perception, and your sense of well-being. Can you identify all the ways you are giving control away to the people or the situation? Think how wonderful it would be if you could move beyond the stress and into a space of honest freedom. Remember the dark cloud. We all have a few of those in our lives. Don't let it hover over you any longer. Get control to get out of its clutches and walk with less stress and worry closing in around you.

Another immediate benefit I have found when regaining control of my life is the way people see me. When you regain control of your life what usually happens is an inner sense of clarity and the knowledge that you have stood up for yourself by creating healthy boundaries. Without you ever saying anything about these internal psychological changes, people around you will sense that you are different. Their interactions and reactions toward you will naturally alter when your thinking alters. Sometimes if it's a controlling relationship, the other person will put up resistance to your changes and test your new boundaries. If you are fortunate and that's not the scenario, then the other person may want to join you in your newfound place of strength and peace. You won't have to invite them, coerce them, manipulate them, or tell them. Moderately healthy people will simply gravitate toward you. Why is this? Because the world is comprised of energy. When yours changes in a positive way, people respond. What you will feel is a heightened dimension of determination, self-belief, strength, and ease of being that you may have never felt before.

As we walk through life, we accumulate baggage of all sorts. Sometimes this baggage is in the form of beliefs. Other times it shows up in patterns of failure, shame, or negative expectations. When you begin to unload this heavy baggage through regaining appropriate control, you will see positive benefits in every area of your life.

Finally, a fourth primary benefit is regaining a clear vision for your future. Our filter can become incredibly skewed. When this happens we lose the vision for our lives that we once had. Where we once were alive, open minded and filled with hope, we may have become beaten down and filled with self-doubt. Regaining control will put you on the path toward your goals and help you clearly define what you want out of life once again.

SHEENA MONNIN

WHY IS NO ONE TALKING ABOUT THIS?

Rebecca was a hard worker. She had steadily climbed up the corporate ladder for over ten years and was proud of her accomplishments. She was meticulous, detailed, organized, and very reliable. Her greatest asset, according to her, was her ability to think clearly and logically under pressure, which was a good thing as her job was inherently filled with pressure and pending deadlines. Rebecca had worked in my client's company for less than a year when I met her. Instantly, I liked her spunk and professionalism. What I didn't know at that time was that a little piece of Rebecca seemed to die each time she interacted with another female in the company.

In my first meeting with Rebecca, we went over the usual leadership assessment and discussed her areas of strength. Everything seemed on par and I was impressed. It wasn't until my second meeting with her that I started to sense her professional veneer was hiding something important from me, something I needed to know in order to best help her reach her personal and professional goals. We began easing our way into discussing the health of the leadership team. Right away, it became apparent what was bothering her. I tried a head-on approach to see if I was correct. Given Rebecca's up-front communication style, I knew she was either going to resist very strongly in not telling me, or was going to be extremely honest in what she thought about this person. Thankfully for both of us, she was honest.

I discovered that Rebecca had been living with pent up frustration for the entire time she had worked at the company. Her co-worker was someone she had to interface with each day, and their decision-making styles could not have been more different. Rebecca felt manipulated, undermined, and controlled. It would have surprised anyone who knew her that beneath the calm professionalism boiled such deeply rooted feelings of manipulation and control. She told me that it was embarrassing for her to talk about her coworker and embarrassing for her to admit that somewhere along the path, she had allowed the woman to influence her emotions and thinking to the degree that she had.

I know that Rebecca isn't alone in her embarrassment and reluctance to admit that she had allowed someone to become her dark cloud, making her feel trapped each time she went to work and making her feel tense whenever a team project came up that involved both of them. It's human nature for most of us to want to fix problems ourselves. It is uncomfortable to admit we need help to understand what is going on and whether or not it is healthy.

On the flip side, when I spoke with Rebecca's coworker in my sessions with her, she felt at peace and confident in her working relationship with Rebecca. A little cockiness even came out as she discussed her interactions with Rebecca. When we become so engrossed in our patterns and when those patterns have been so deeply reinforced, it's common to no longer see fault with them at first glance. Usually it takes a long time of committed effort to begin to see the error of our ways if we have slid into the role of controller or manipulator.

As for Rebecca, she became gradually more satisfied at work when we discussed how she could regain control over her thoughts and emotions and begin to erect barriers in her life once again.

The broader point here is this: even though it is very uncomfortable to admit when things are flying out of control, or even when they are crawling out of control, it's important to seek the help you need if you are unable to break the cycle yourself.

Just as when we discussed the concept of victimhood and why people play the victim, there is also a theme in society that encourages business professionals to keep their problems to themselves. Thankfully, I'm seeing a positive trend in the importance that companies are putting on the psychological health of their employees. In the 1950's, for example, I've heard stories of how, in the eyes of the company, saying you have seen a psychologist was the same as saying you had an incurable, infectious disease. Today, that mindset is changing. More people are willing to talk about their problems and learn how they can appropriately make changes to correct those problems.

~§~
There is a balance that needs to be reached between the two extremes.
~§~

I would never advocate someone holding their fears, pain, and heartache inside without ever sharing them. I would also not encourage someone to persist in trumpeting their weaknesses and struggles while denying personal responsibility or claiming to be a victim of life. Neither extreme is healthy. Neither extreme makes for a good friend, spouse, or coworker.

Another reason people probably don't like talking about the loss of control in their lives is that inevitably it will involve another person, often someone close to them. While there are some exceptions, most of us don't enjoy blasting negativity around about other people. It seems to heighten our loss of control in the moment and it makes us feel weak, or even mean. This is understandable. I'm not a fan of admitting when I have allowed someone to control me, and I do not enjoy the reality of needing to express factually what has occurred in order to fix the problem and regain control. I also don't enjoy having to relive the unpleasant experiences with the purpose of resolving them. Old triggers become reactivated and often the overwhelming emotions of past experiences feel brand new and filled with the same or more intensified emotions. The process of talking about our loss of control may not be enjoyable, but the result is the freedom of moving beyond the situation.

In many professional arenas, once you admit someone has crossed a line with you, some sort of confrontation will need to take place. Even when a third party like myself is involved, if the situation has reached the level of negativity that warrants intervention, it is likely that both parties will be aware of the opinions and accusations of the other. Knowing this will be the case, more than a few people shy away from the act of talking about what has happened. Again, you must believe that the need to regain control is more important than your temporary discomfort.

One point I drove home to Rebecca is to learn to recognize the signs of when you are giving ground away. This is true in the professional world as well as in your personal life.

What did Rebecca's coworker specifically do to make Rebecca feel controlled and manipulated? Truthfully, it was difficult for Rebecca to even remember at first. Often when someone is being a bully or trying to control you, their methods are not easy to put into words. Their methods may not even be overt or traceable.

Rebecca left our session and went to her email and texts, looking for menacing or bossy messages. Nothing was there. By the time our follow-up session arrived, she had all but talked herself out of the possibility that she had indeed been legitimately manipulated and controlled. She backpedaled and seemed unsure what to think. I had taken good notes and we referred to those, bringing back to light the truth of her feelings the day she had shared them with me. If Rebecca had chosen to deny the problem, her situation would not have changed for the better. It would have become worse as she stuffed her feelings and thoughts away into the recess of her subconscious. As it was, she wrote down a few affirmations to herself that included how she would not allow her coworker to control her any longer, and she did her best to remain in reality, not in denial, about the situation.

When something has been buried for a long time, it's common to not want to share it. It's even more common to share it and then start to become afraid because of the vulnerability of having opened up about feelings that have been buried for a long time. The most common way to stop feeling vulnerable is to deny that anything is wrong. If I encounter someone who has established a base level of honesty and open sharing with me, and then suddenly starts to become overly positive or absolutely avoidant of someone or something, I know I've hit a trigger and I need to tread carefully. If you feel denial or self-doubt creep in upon sharing or even thinking about sharing a controlling situation with someone, rest assured that is a normal feeling. Push through the fear and see it through to the end.

Like Rebecca, you may be in a controlling situation that is subtle. It may not involve threatening letters or horrible messages written on the wall in a back room. It may be as simple as being routinely cut off when trying to speak or being belittled by a word or a look. Over time, this type of bullying behavior does take its toll. If you are repeatedly being sent the message that you are a failure, that you aren't important, or that your ideas are horrible, eventually your brain will begin to send messages of frustration or doubt to your conscious mind. The only trace you will have to prove your point of being mistreated is the record of your feelings or a gradual change in the freedom and self-confidence you once felt. Now is not the time to doubt the validity of your feelings. You don't need physical proof to convince yourself that you have fallen into an unhealthy cycle of control. Take action today and work to rebuild appropriate boundaries where you are.

.

STANDING UP FOR YOURSELF VERSUS CONTROLLING OTHERS

The concept of having rights is a universal principle. In some countries having rights is fully explored, explained, and expected. In other countries the concept is still evolving. For us as individuals, we decide each day if we have rights, what they are, and how they are defined.

What is a right? It's something—an action, object, principle, etc.—generally believed to be something we are *entitled* to. It's not necessarily a privilege, though some would define certain rights that way. Rights are generally not supposed to be subjective, based on anything about us, whether or not we deserve the right or whether or not we have earned it. Rights are resolute, unyielding, and often protected by law.

Sometimes we have rights that we aren't aware of, or that have been taken away and we've forgotten them. Other times, we take our own rights away through our beliefs and thoughts.

A friend of mine is a musician. He told me one of the greatest lessons he learned years before when he was just starting out forming a band was how to lead people without resorting to criticism over repeated errors. He shared a story with me about how he used to become frustrated with his band members who weren't getting a certain part of the song the way he wanted them to. On one particularly trying day of frustration, he called out one of the guys and berated him a bit in front of the band, ending by saying he was going to keep an eye on him. No one contradicted my friend. Because of this, he continued to criticize and get away with it. Weeks went by with this type of leadership style being enforced anytime something went wrong. What he discovered was that instead of becoming better, the band was becoming worse. And none of the members seemed to want to be there. One day in the middle of several critical remarks, he stopped, actually listening to his own words. That was a wake up call for him. From that day on he stopped leading like a dictator and started leading the way he would want to be led.

What happened to the band members? They gave their right to be treated with basic respect away. At the first infraction, one of them should have put a stop to it, but no one did. As a pattern developed, the early opportunity to correct the wrong came and went as all the people involved became accustomed to the way the interaction occurred. No one in the band liked the interaction, but they still adopted a certain level of acceptance that negatively impacted them all.

Have you heard the term 'groupthink' before? It's a fairly common psychological term that refers to a group of people, or a team, that is more concerned with maintaining the group or team's unified front than it is with making objectively good decisions. In short, groupthink is displayed when I am putting more value on my team working cohesively together than I am on making quality, long term, beneficial decisions. If we are so focused on acting like a well-connected group that we forget to seek outside opinions or look at our goals from a realistic, well researched perspective, it's possible that the group will fall into groupthink and the result will be everyone actively working toward something or deeply believing something that is not grounded in reality or particularly healthy.

Another aspect of groupthink is losing your own identity for the sake of the group. If you've ever read the book 'Call of the Wild' by Jack London, you know how a pack of wolves operates. You know the hierarchy within the pack and you know that no one leaves their spot without challenging and ultimately either killing or kicking out the leader of the pack. The leader has absolute authority and the pack follows the leader generally without resistance. Wolf packs are a great example of groupthink. The pack trusts the lead wolf with their very lives. The pack ceases to be a group of individuals who have their own hunting and breeding ideas and instead becomes an extension of the lead wolf.

I see this at times in teams in the workplace. If the leader (manager, owner, CEO) is off the charts in their personality type as dominant, aggressive, or bold in decision-making, usually the team will follow with few challenges to the 'lead wolf'. Group think occurs not because the team doesn't have their own ideas or opinions, but because the energy of the leader is so domineering that the group prefers to keep their thoughts to themselves in order to not be called out and potentially rebuked for offering an alternative perspective. This style of leadership can only last so long before someone in the team stands up and either walks out or gathers their nerve enough to confront the unhealthy leader. I'd encourage you, if you find yourself feeling like one of the pack with no voice and no freedom of expression to take an action step and remove yourself from the groupthink mentality. It's not healthy to be repressed and it's not healthy for the domineering leader to be able to persist in unhealthy dominance over others.

It could be that you are in a groupthink position and only just now are awakening to the reality that you have given yards of your tug-of-war rope away. You may feel vulnerable thinking about how much ground you've lost. You may feel angry with yourself. You may already be slipping back into denial that there's even a problem. I'm not advocating one bold move on your part to extricate yourself from the situation. But I am advocating consistent, stubborn steps on your part to regain healthy boundaries and remember how valuable your voice is.

Just like in the previous example of the band members, all it takes is one change from a group member to make the entire group different. In that case it was actually the leader who changed. But in your case, it could be you who changes, and the ripple effect can be huge. Frankly, I don't know what the band members were thinking or why they decided it was okay for their founding member and leader to speak down to them in an inappropriate manner. Looking at it from the outside, even with as little detail as we have, it's obvious that the band members let go of the tug-of-war rope and lost ground.

I get it, though, that at times we can lose perspective of what is appropriate control and what is going too far. And the truth is, there isn't a clear-cut formula to help us fully determine the difference. Each scenario is different. What is too much for a passive personality type may be just right for a more aggressive type.

A little while ago we talked about being self-aware. This practice of self-awareness will greatly change our lives if we build it into a habit.

~§~
Self-awareness is the first step toward becoming in tune with your own boundaries as well as when you may be infringing upon someone else's rights.
~§~

On a scale of 1-10, with 1 being 'never' and 10 being 'frequently', how self-aware are you each day? Self-awareness sounds simple when it's defined. It's noticing your moods, thoughts, beliefs, reactions, and tendencies and consciously taking ownership of them. This not only prevents problems (something I am a fan of) but it also leads to stronger working relationships and the ability to stay focused as a leader (benefits that may resonate with you).

Each day, notice these and similar behaviors that demonstrate a *lack* of self-awareness to monitor yourself:

- Judging a situation before you experience it
- Reacting verbally without considering the ramifications
- Not sensing when others' nonverbal cues are shifting
- Repeated thoughts that are not beneficial or true
- Forgetting what was said only a short time before
- Tuning people out or being unduly preoccupied

After we conquer the initial challenges of becoming self-aware, we can be free to focus on how aware we are of others. This leads us into a new section that discusses what has the ability to control us.

SECTION TWO

WHAT HAS THE ABILITY TO CONTROL US?

OUR BELIEFS, THOUGHTS, FEELINGS

The classic TV series, *The Andy Griffith Show*, has a popular episode about how important our beliefs are and how they influence our actions and interactions with others.

Opie, Andy's son, seemingly tells a lie. Andy catches Opie telling this apparent lie and is flabbergasted. The school was collecting money from the children in pennies or nickels for a clothing drive. Opie repeatedly said he didn't have any money to give. The teacher hinted to Andy that Opie was the only child who hadn't done anything to help with the clothing drive. Andy confronted Opie and his son staunchly said he didn't have any money to give. Andy recounted Opie's allowance and how much candy Opie must have eaten to have spent it all. Opie still refused to give money. Andy was disappointed in his son's seeming stinginess. Opie felt betrayed by his dad's lack of faith in him. Finally, at the end of the episode we learn that Opie had met a little girl who needed a coat. He sincerely didn't have any money to give to the school collection because he was saving it bit by bit to buy her a coat. Andy had believed the voice in his mind telling him that his son was lying rather than believed the word of his son, temporarily causing a breach in their relationship.

~§~
Our beliefs are powerful. They influence us in both good and bad ways.
~§~

Something similar happened to me not too long ago. I was told years ago that cardio wasn't as important as weight training. Never one to be a fan of cardio, I believed the expert who was telling me this. As a result, I have adamantly defended myself when refusing friends and family who have wanted to start running and asked me to join them. I said more times than I can count that there was no need for me to run. I was doing quite enough with regularly lifting weights in the gym. I believed what I'd been told without question and, true to form, wanted to avoid any potential discomfort from running. It was only recently that a new voice challenged me and I saw the situation from a different angle. The truth is, there are a myriad of benefits to running regularly. I started to focus on the benefits to my overall health and decided to take the plunge. I found out that my beliefs all these years had been errant. They weren't true. I had believed the words of a supposed expert and had not fully tested the theory that an entirely new set of benefits could come if I added cardio to my workout routine.

Beliefs are like carrots: all we see is the top part, the leafy greens, sticking out of the ground, but underneath the soil the root is deep and strong. It takes a little work to find the root of our beliefs and even more effort to analyze whether the belief is true or not. When you do analyze the root, and you see the truth as I saw about my denial of needing to run long distances, you'll probably wish you'd stopped to analyze your belief sooner. I have found over the years that the more I explore my beliefs and my patterns, the more of them I get rid of, or, at the very least, alter. Life is not stagnant. I've said that before. The truth of that statement can be one of the most liberating things in your life.

Over the centuries there have been old beliefs held true by nations, tribes, and huge organizations of people that were finally overturned to welcome a new belief. Several global issues have come into being simply due to an errant belief. We don't often think of the impact our beliefs have on our lives and the lives of those around us, but the impact is apparent. Old wives tales of throwing salt over your shoulder or not walking under a ladder or the significance of encountering a black cat are not necessarily something to laugh at if they have become a belief that influences you. Superstitions that incite fear or misplaced loyalty can hold great power over us. I've found that doing independent research when I have a doubt about a belief I'm holding to be true is a good way to check boundaries and see what you're giving your power away to.

Beliefs don't just spring out of thin air. They are bred in our minds. They are born of us agreeing with a thought. Our thoughts have the ability to transform our mood from sour to ecstatic. From ungrateful to munificent. From 'I could never accomplish that' to 'I can do this'.

It's astounding to consider how much power we give away to the thoughts that we think. If these thoughts are healthy, then this is not a bad thing. But if the thoughts are feeding the dark cloud or are causing us to lose our grip on the tug-of-war rope then we need to stop immediately and self assess.

Have you ever had a miscommunication with someone and they responded with, 'Well, I thought you said that'? If we think someone told us something and we act on that thought, it could get us into some trouble. Being a good listener can help to clarify our thoughts and keep us from developing unintended beliefs that could harm us.

Even more fleeting than thoughts are our feelings. The imprints our feelings leave on us are even more profound than our thoughts and beliefs, though the feelings may be fleeting. This is because there is a great intertwining power of association between the feelings we have and thoughts they evoke. Think of the last relationship you were in. How many feelings did you have about that person in the beginning? Too many to remember, right? Of all those feelings, I'd imagine most of them were positive, maybe even unrealistically positive. Your filter was skewed by your feelings and your thoughts were skewed by the filter. As a result, you probably initially thought that person was the greatest thing ever to happen in your life. Fast-forward several months. Did the person change? Probably not. Did your thoughts about them change? Likely. Why? Because your feelings cooled down enough to *not* alter the reality before you. You could more clearly see the reality of the other person. It happens all the time. Our emotions tell us life is perfect one day, and the next, we question everything we once felt so acutely as reality.

~§~
If you are going to rely on something steadfast to keep you on track in life, try not to make this measuring rod your feelings.
~§~

A better approach is to use a combination of good beliefs, accurate thoughts, and a little bit of emotion thrown together. If we rely on one only, we are missing 2/3's of the picture. Life is better lived with a solid combination of the three together.

OUR EXPECTATIONS

Why do married couples harbor resentment against each other? I'm not talking about the huge anger-filled, knockout arguments. I'm talking about the little resentments that slowly eat at you until you secretly despise quite a few things about your spouse.

The answer is so simple that it's shocking. And we do this every single day from the moment we wake up until the moment we go to bed. We do it in traffic on our way to work. We persist doing it while we are at work. We do it with our kids and with our friends. We even do it with ourselves in our own minds. We do it with loved ones and we do it with strangers we encounter once and will never see again.

I'm talking about creating and nurturing our expectations.

Expectations put us in bondage and keep us in bondage, creating havoc and mayhem with each relationship we have. Expectations feed our ego and create an inner judge and jury mentality that pushes people away and eternally frustrates us. Those around us *will* 'fail' us. And you know what? *We will fail others, too.*

One of the heaviest burdens to carry around psychologically (outside of more serious issues like abuse, betrayal, etc.) is the burden of consistently unfulfilled expectations. Day after day, with each infraction against the expectations we have erected as measuring rods in our minds for success and perfection, we add more baggage. Time after time, as people fail to reach the standard we believe they need to reach, our disappointment and disapproval is reinforced. Before we know it, we are bitter. We become short tempered. We get upset frequently and feel like the burden of keeping all aspects of our family and job and life in line has been loaded upon our shoulders. That, my friend, is not healthy. That is a burden far too heavy for you to have to carry. In the end, it will crush your spirit and it will imprint you with stress you were never intended to have to experience.

The world will keep rotating without your help. Your family will eventually remember to put their dirty clothes in the hamper...sometimes. The erratic drivers in rush hour traffic will likely continue to drive erratically whether or not you are upset and choose to give them a lecture they'll never hear while you follow them down the road. Your coworker may still leave a mess behind them in the break room, though you've made it clear a dozen times that they need to clean up after themselves. Your children may not behave perfectly in the store or ace every test or win every athletic award. And you, *even you*, will fall short a time or two by forgetting the dry cleaning or mailing out a birthday card a couple of days too late.

All of these things and many more may still occur each day until you die. And you know what? It's not always your problem to bear. It's not always your business to turn your critical eye toward those people and seek to control them by fixing them or lecturing them or holding an attitude against them. That's right, by allowing your expectations to control your thoughts you, in turn, become the bully by taking other people's rights away. We are all capable of this. I've personally carried the weight of correctness on my shoulders far to frequently to have anything less than an understanding ear and an empathetic mentality for those who believe no one can function without their help, or those who believe that by constantly keeping the standard of excellence so high, people will be inspired to continue to strive toward the standard.

Can I confide in you what I've learned? People don't always care about *our* standards. In fact, people are free beings and they are perfectly able to set their own standard and live by it. *And I have to learn to be okay with that.*

Again, I'm not talking about the deep, foundational principles of respect, trust, and integrity. Those are the absolutes that you create early on in any relationship. I'm talking about the smaller preferences that some of us believe are carved in stone and must be adhered to, no matter what.

So often, long term personal or working relationships are wrought with angst and bitterness simply because the small issues have become so LARGE. Instead of seeing the person we once liked and respected, all we now see are the issues, the flaws, and the irritants. Something as simple as not putting the cereal box back in its proper place each morning can become an all-consuming issue that tears an otherwise good marriage apart.

I'm very involved in Toastmasters International, a public speaking group with clubs worldwide. Each year, a speech contest is held, with participants from around the world working their way through higher levels until a world champion is declared. Contestants who win at the club level progress to increasing levels of competition until they potentially reach the international stage. One year a woman gave a speech that was jaw dropping in its truth and depth of message. It was about her first marriage and her inflated expectations, and how these ruined her marriage.

She started the speech by revealing how young she was when she was married and how much she really loved her first husband. They were a happy, active couple with big ideas for their careers and their future. After the honeymoon period was over, little differences started coming out. Typical for all of us. She was an organized, methodical, non-emotional wife. He was more sensitive, withdrawn, and a very deep thinker. She talked more. He talked less. She was a neat freak. He was a slob, according to her. Why did she consider him a slob? Two things—and two things only—created this false perception of him in her mind. He left the milk out in the morning after making his favorite bowl of cereal, and he put all his clothes in the hamper except for his socks. They always seemed to end up on the floor beside the dirty clothes hamper. True story. These two things bothered her so much that eventually she began to leave notes on the refrigerator and taped above the hamper to remind him to do things the 'right way', which actually just meant 'her way'. A few years later, the expectations of tidiness still firmly in place, they decided to end their marriage. Both partners were frustrated, tired, and stressed. Both partners thought the other person was the problem. There had been no affair, no irresponsible use of their money by either person, and no mean words or threats. They simply believed they weren't as compatible as they first thought.

The speech hit home to a lot of people in the audience because the prevalence of unbalanced expectations among all of us is high. I'll ask you this: what are your expectations worth to you? Is it worth losing your marriage? Is it worth alienating your kids or your extended family? It is worth the stress inherent with this type of behavior? I hope you don't believe that it is.

~§~
Our preferences generally dictate our expectations.
~§~

I prefer that you not talk so loud while we are out at a restaurant. Yet, you continue to speak loud enough for others around us to hear what our conversation is about. My expectation is that you will respect our privacy. Your expectation is that I will allow you the freedom of expression and freedom to become passionate about what you are saying to the point that your voice increases in volume.

Our expectations collide. What should we do?

Or, I prefer that you not slam the door for the millionth time when you're coming in from the garage. Why do I prefer this? I can't even explain it, but it irritates me when you slam the door, *so stop doing it!* However, you always come in from work with your hands full and you use your foot to whack the door closed. Perhaps in your mind, you would prefer that your job not require you to bring so much home that you have to either make two trips from the car or must lug it all in at once, and as a result, slam the door. Most people will not explain their thinking early on. They will secretly grumble when an expectation is violated, thus reinforcing their skewed belief that their expectation is the only valid option or opinion.

Truly, your expectation for these types of preferences is *not* the only valid option, opinion, belief, or need. The other person's voice matters, too. Don't let your expectations remain buried inside. Talk about them when appropriate, or, in the workplace, if it is not appropriate, monitor your thoughts surrounding the expectation and begin to let go of the negativity. You may be so deeply entrenched in unfulfilled expectations that you feel justified to judge others with each infraction. By simply starting to realize that your way is not the *only correct way*, you will be on the first step of your journey toward freedom from this type of control. If you don't want your expectations to control you, do something about it today, and every day.

What do I do, though, when my expectations clearly collide with someone else's expectations, someone I have to either live with or interact with each day? If the relationship is healthy enough, you can discuss your expectations. Avoid using judgmental words or accusatory score-keeping words. Before the conversation, remind yourself that you'll get nowhere in the discussion if you are still stubbornly believing that your expectations are the only valid option. Get rid of that obstinacy and welcome the notion that the person you are about to speak with is just that: a person. And as a person they are flawed, they have triggers, they have opinions, and they have habits, just as you also have all of those things.

If the relationship is not healthy, then the work will fall to you, especially at first. For those who are so deeply wedded to their unhealthy expectations, it might be helpful to think of each expectation as a jail cell, like the one in the *Monopoly* game. Each time the other person lands in jail by not living up to the expectation, you can reach into your stack of playing cards and pull out a 'get out of jail free' card. The visual can be helpful, but even more helpful is starting to embrace the idea that if you don't give them this 'get out of jail free' card, then your expectations are controlling you. By pulling out the card and giving it to them, you are forcing yourself to step outside the prison you unknowingly are in and choosing to control your expectations of others. It's difficult at first, and some people can only produce 2 or 3 cards in a day. But over time, those unhealthy expectations will lose their grip and you can be firmly in the driver's seat of your life once again.

Reality TV is still very popular, though most every topic imaginable has been filmed and aired. One of the earlier of these shows was the show 'The Biggest Loser', about people wanting to lose a significant amount of weight and regain control of their life. One of the most eye-opening exercises the people on the show had to endure came after they'd lost about 50 pounds. They were taken outside near a sandy hill. They were told to run up the slight incline, which most of them could do without a problem. Then they were told to run up it again, but this time with all the extra weight that they'd recently lost. They were essentially chained to their extra weight and had to drag it up the hill. It was exhausting and it was eye opening because they had already become accustomed to not carrying the extra weight around. When it was added back into their lives, they were surprised at how difficult everything was, and how much happier they were without having to carry it around every day.

It's the same for us. We are carrying pounds and pounds of extra baggage through life because of our expectations and we don't even realize it. But if you stay with these concepts and start to get rid of extra weight, you will be amazed by how much easier, happier, and healthier life is.

SHEENA MONNIN

OUR IDENTITY, NEEDS, REACTIONS, ENVIRONMENT

Lorie was a super mom, a super wife, a super sister, and a super member of all the kids' school clubs, rallies, and fundraisers. She seemed to have boundless energy and could do it all. Her husband was super intellectual, super quick witted, and a super provider for the family. It seems like the perfect combination at first glance. In fact, it was a healthy combination for eighteen years of marriage. Each member of the family had their place and their roles and responsibilities were solidified. Then, the eldest child flew out of the nest and attended college in another state. The dynamic changed somewhat but there were still four children at home and life continued to move on. When the second child left for college the dynamic changed drastically. Suddenly there were considerably fewer tasks to be done and obligations to handle. Lorie felt her world changing in ways she wasn't sure she knew how to control. She sought more group activities and began to travel in a volunteer position for an international group. Her husband was baffled why his happy, outgoing wife was leaving their three youngest children (all in high school) behind and pursuing a newfound interest that involved travel.

When Lorie was home she was just as engaged as ever, but when she was gone the entire family felt it, particularly her husband. His needs for emotional companionship were not being met. Her need of being a super mom had shifted and been put on the backburner where it stewed until it nearly boiled over. You see, with the changes in the family dynamics, Lorie's identity was changing. To her, it was not challenging to be a super mom to three kids. She felt empty without the constant 'on-the-go' she had enjoyed for so many years. As an extravert, her one-on-one companionship needs were minimal compared to her husband. They each had valid needs but were inadvertently allowing those needs to control them, to drive them apart instead of working to solve the problem and bring them both closer together. As Lorie's identity shifted from being involved in elementary, middle, and high school all at once to suddenly just having a few high school clubs and groups to run, she didn't know how to process it.

I see this often when a long time businessperson is facing retirement. Work of any type can become our primary identity card, the way we see ourselves and the way we explain ourselves to others. If that is taken away or adjusted beyond what we are ready for or comfortable with, then all the feelings, fears, doubt, and anxiety associated with the change will begin to control us, changing our behaviors and our actions.

Lorie's story doesn't end there, though. As time went on and yet a third child went off to college, her travel position went from volunteer to paying. She had not yet processed what was driving her to take the position and all the unhappy emotions associated with several huge life changes that had occurred within a short time span. When the opportunity of a new identity came up, her unprocessed needs leaped at the chance of a new image. She was busy again, and she loved it. Her husband continued to hold down the fort at home when she was gone and gradually grew to enjoy the solitude the changes had brought into his routine. He read more books that he'd been meaning to read and he took the dogs for long walks through fields and woods. He remembered how pleasant it was for him to not be always going to a high school game or summer camp. His world became relaxing and filled with quiet activities he enjoyed. Eventually, the inevitable happened. Lorie became burnt out. She started staying home more, and with her presence back in the house, all the unmet needs of the two of them made their life together difficult.

Over time, they began to work things out. And in the process, they learned a valuable lesson that many of us can apply to our own lives. They saw how easily our needs could control us and drive us to do things we would not rationally do. Lorie's need to be important drove her away from her family for a while. Her husband's needs for companionship became buried as he convinced himself he was enjoying his solitude more than his spunky, energetic wife. Unearthing these very different needs was challenging. Exploring how tied Lorie was to a certain identity and image took even more work.

You and I have identity needs as well. We have emotional needs. In the above story, both the husband and wife had legitimate needs, although the needs weren't necessarily unhealthy at first. If we don't take the time to explore what is missing from our lives or how changes in life are influencing our level of satisfaction and happiness, we can lose control and our relationships will suffer.

If you look at long-term professional or personal relationships, you can usually see with ease whose needs are more dominant, and as a result, whose needs are being met more regularly. Look at Lorie, for example. Her need to be important was being met. She saw to that. But her husband's need was silent and overlooked. The more the pattern of putting Lorie's need first became reinforced, the more difficult it was to change the pattern into something balanced and healthy.

Take a minute and consider what needs you believe you have in your life. In your quest to get those needs met, how much control are you giving away to the need?

Needs are, sincerely, like weeds. Now, I'm not saying that having needs is bad. Each of us has valid needs that must be met. The problem is, sometimes we focus on our needs so much we allow them to grow in size and spread across our lives until they choke out the good parts of our relationships. If left unattended, our unmet needs can become more and more demanding. They can even blossom into new needs that mask the original ones, and they can dominate the fertile soil of our emotions. How? Unmet needs can make us unkind, less than thoughtful, and difficult to reach emotionally. They tend to make us resentful, touchy, and self-focused. As they replace our true identity, they cause us to lose sight of what is really important in our lives.

~§~
It is important to remember that not all needs are healthy and valid.
~§~

A great number of people hide their controlling tendencies behind the disguise of an unmet need that others are obligated to cater to. Being around people who may be pushing their needs on us naturally awakens our reactions to their behaviors.

Would you consider yourself to be a reactive person? Or are you more prone to sit quietly and ponder things completely through in your mind rather than quickly responding? If you answered 'yes' to the first question, this next part of the chapter is for you. If you answered 'yes' to the second question, this next part of the chapter is still for you because there are far more reactive people in the world than non-reactive people.

I'm a reactive person. When things are clear to me, I can speak quickly and passionately, and will stand by my words no matter what. Very rarely do I change my mind or alter my course once I am convinced of my direction. I can also be non-reactive when a situation arises and I don't have a quick answer to it in my mind. In those instances, I withdraw to ponder my course of action. When I decide on my path, I then charge forward and can react and respond quickly and decisively. For me, it all depends on knowing where I am going. If I lose my direction, it is apparent to those who know me because I fail to speak strongly and sometimes I grow quiet for long periods of time.

If you are a reactive person, that means that no sooner does someone finish a thought or sentence than you are opening your mouth with some input—either to counter what they said or support it. Reactive people are 'live wires', meaning there's always a current running through their brains, and there is usually a compulsion to share that current with others through bold and passionate self-expression.

If you are non-reactive, most often you will be calm. You listen to what people are saying and try to discern their intention. You will want to take the time to research your answers, and you may check out mentally and emotionally from conversations and situations.

Though very different in nature, both approaches can be controlling factors in your day. If we allow our quick reactions to override our rational mind, then we are giving ground away that we need to regain. If we take too long to withdraw and process information, then we are also giving ground away by allowing the lack of reaction to rob us of being present in the moment and engaging the experience by voicing our opinions. Seeking balance between the two approaches will eradicate any form of control your reactions may have over you.

When I was a little girl I used to love summer camp. I looked forward all year to going to camp, staying in the cabins, learning outdoor skills such as archery, field sports, and basketball. I loved sitting around the campfire with all the older girls and wishing I could look as pretty as they were or be as cool as the most popular girls were. All the pre-teen dreams we girls dream were alive and living in my heart and mind. One year, I went to camp and realized I had graduated. I was put in the older girls' cabin along with my good friend who came to camp with me. It was one of the most exciting events in my life up until that point. I was ecstatic and so was my friend. We stayed quiet most of the time, soaking in their older girls 'teenage wisdom' and hearing stories of their escapades about getting their learner's permit to drive, or having their braces taken off, or being allowed to finally wear makeup. My friend and I listened wide-eyed, dying to one day be as experienced in life as the older girls. To us, getting a learner's permit seemed a million years away, and yes, both of us still had braces on our teeth.

When my friend and I returned home after camp, something about us had changed. The true us had not changed, but the influence of our environment temporarily altered how we spoke, the slang words we used, and even how we walked. We had not fully realized the impact the older girls had on us until both our parents sat us down for a talk. They told us to enjoy life as a pre-teen and not to rush the growing up process. They pointed out several ways our attitudes and behaviors had changed. In about a week, the romantic view we'd had of the older girls was abandoned as we built forts in the woods by our houses and rode bikes and wrote plays we thought for sure would be turned into something real one day.

The memory of that particular summer camp has stayed with me because, as an adult, I can more fully appreciate the heavy influence our environment has on us, no matter what our age. My friend and I weren't engaging in 'groupthink', but we were allowing our environment to have control over us. Each day, each of us moves from environment to environment, from home to work, from work to dinner, from dinner to back home again. Throw in a few social clubs or groups and you have a long list of potentially controlling environments.

If you feel yourself changing after being around certain people or in certain groups, take the time to analyze why. Maybe you're trying to people please. Or maybe the group's influence is so strong that you have failed to see the control it has over you. Until now. Today is the day to decide if you want your environment to be able to manipulate you and change you without your permission.

OUR DREAMS, PASSIONS, DESIRES

When you were a child, what did you want to do when you grew up?
For some, perhaps it was to be a teacher or an attorney. For others, it
may have been to be just like a parent or a grandparent, maybe going
into business or politics or engineering. Most children have more
than one idea of what they want their future job to be, even if they
weren't raised in an environment where the dreams of the future are
nourished and encouraged. Children dream.

The question is, can our dreams control us? Can the failure to
reach these dreams affect our mind, our heart, and our sense of
value?

I heard the story once of a little boy who was great at baseball. He
was naturally talented and his presence on the field amazing for one
so young. He was assigned to be the pitcher for the local team from
the time he began playing the sport. His arm was 'made to throw',
some people said. He was successful with each team he played on,
and by the time he was a teenager, he had caught the eye of more
than a few scouts. He was asked to join a special group of up-and-
coming baseball talents at a summer baseball camp.

This was his moment. For years he had wanted this, prepared for it, and dreamed about it. Every time he scanned the signed memorabilia from the baseball games he had attended while growing up, he was reminded of one driving force in his life—all he wanted to do was to play professional baseball. Now, years of work were about to either pay off…or not.

He performed decently well at the camp and was asked to attend a second, even more exclusive, camp. The guys in this camp were the best of the best. The pressure was immense. The competition, fierce. The young man in our story choked up. He could feel the fear building and the pressure getting to him, but he wouldn't talk about it because he couldn't admit that his dream was slowly starting to slip away. He began to fail. He began to miss the mark. Instead of confiding in someone and getting his fears out in the open, he held them in as they turned into anger.

Visions of his brothers practicing with him and his mom faithfully driving him to and from each game or practice clouded his focus. They had done those things for him, for his dream—the dream he had nurtured almost all of his life. By the end of that summer, his dream was dead. He hadn't made the cut. He had been reprimanded multiple times for verbal mistreatment of the other prospects attending the camp and ultimately sent home.

I can't imagine the conversation that day with his family. He was a teenager with a good arm, an arm made for pitching, but nowhere to pitch and no other opportunities. He went on to have a successful career in the military, earning one honor and distinction after another. But the dream of the past haunted him. And it continued to be a sore topic for him. No amount of success in other areas of his life could make up for the death of his first real dream. He lived under the dark cloud of disappointment, failure, and the memory of everything he used to want, but never received.

Dreams aren't always career related. The dreams we have for our lives can be certain financial milestones, the type of spouse we will have, or how many children we want, where we want to live or the type of car we want to drive. Our dreams come in endless varieties and having a dream is not a bad thing. If we fail to attain the dream and it starts to haunt us or cause us shame, then we have crossed the line into an unhealthy area. The dream has begun to control us.

Briefly, I took ballet lessons as a young adult. My instructor tried to be kind and supportive, but deep in her heart she was bitter. She was excellent at finding flaws and correcting them in her students, which is important in something as detailed as ballet, but there was underlying tension with her everywhere she went. Often when I arrived early, I would find her with her hand on the bar, trying to strike a graceful ballet pose high on her toes. The pain in her face as her ankle and arthritic toes betrayed her was difficult to watch. Slowly, she would lower herself down onto the heels of her feet and sigh. Her mouth would grow taut and the light in her eyes would dim a little more. Her body had failed her. And she was not yet 45-years-old. I was surprised when one day she let a comment slip about how she had been injured years before and become unable to perform for a well-known ballet company. The nature of her injury left her in constant pain. Her dream had died. She felt her world was shattered.

We all have choices to make when bad things happen. We can choose to allow our dreams to manipulate us emotionally, constantly comparing our current life to the one we once believed we would live. We can allow the hurt and disappointment to return to our mind again and again, shooting poison darts of worthlessness, failure, shame, and self-anger at us, driving our bitterness or sense of ineptness ever deeper into our psyche. Both examples above are true. Both people never quite regained control of their lives after their initial dreams died before their eyes.

Sometimes circumstances out of our control will stop our dreams from coming true. Other times, our decisions will block them. When this happens, a very common aftereffect begins to take shape. Soon, the dark cloud of regret takes the reins of our life away from us and starts to turn us in directions that aren't healthy for us. Regret is a powerful, insidious emotion. It limits us and puts pressure on us— pressure that is often too great for us to handle. When we lose the battle with regret, we tend to withdraw from people and our clear mind becomes cloudy. Our filter stops speaking truth to us, and instead we begin to interpret everything around us through the memories of the regrets we have. Our self-esteem suffers, and we can lash out at others without intending to. People stop seeming like they are on our side. It feels like they are out to get us.

Whatever the situation, we can choose to remain strong in our minds. We can decide every day, every hour, every minute if necessary, that we will not succumb to thoughts of self-hatred, self-pity, or denial. The young man in our first example tried the approach of denial multiple times, but in the quietest moments of the day, he felt a tidal wave of pain wash over him. That was how strongly his dream had burned within him. Denial will only work for so long before the truth of our emotions bursts through its thin veneer. A great many people walk around barely keeping a lid on the ocean of pain within, barely able to survive the gnawing reality of a failed past. One of the hardest things to do is to admit that you have baggage to process in this area, to admit that you failed in a huge way and that you may need to take all those memories out and examine them. But you do need to examine them or you will never be able to release them so they can't control you anymore.

~§~
One primary way of starting this process is to
replace self-condemnation with a word of truth.
~§~

Blanket statements that float around in our minds are rarely good. Things like the following examples are warning signs for us that we have lost some balance in our lives: 'You don't deserve that promotion.' Or 'Why would anyone hire you? You know people don't really like you.' Or 'Of course you failed. Again. Why act surprised?' Or 'If anyone found out what you did that summer…they'd kick you to the curb.'

In the case of the ballet instructor, she had slipped into several of those types of self-condemnation. Most of them weren't true, and they were robbing her of a free life filled with peace.

~§~
We can have as much peace as we choose to have. Remove the cobwebs of broken dreams from your mind to begin to walk in peace today.
~§~

What is deeply tied to our dreams? What energy is wrapped around and throughout each dream we hold sacred to our hearts? Our emotional passion.

Be careful where you let your passion take you.

Just because you have a dream fueled by passion does not mean that dream is realistic or healthy for you. Take the time to think through your passions and determine which are helping you in life and which are detracting from you living your very best life each day. You must control your passions as far as your dreams are concerned, because if you don't, they will start to direct you down paths that may not be best for you and can only end in failure.

Smaller than our dreams and passions but equally important are our daily desires.

If I were to meet you and ask you to tell me three things you desire, could you do it? I think you could likely list considerably more than three things. I know that I can. Our mind tells us each day what we desire. For instance, I may desire a certain type of specially prepared lunch or a certain style of car. I may desire to reach a certain income bracket or desire to be a certain size or lift a certain weight in the gym. If you stop to consider your list, it's apparent that your desires take you where they want you to go each day. They push and pull you to perhaps spend too much, or hold tightly to each dollar you make. They lead you to certain activities and hobbies.

~§~
Keeping our desires under control is an important daily exercise,
one that helps us to remain focused on the bigger picture.
~§~

Desires can be fleeting, diverting you from more important paths. They can be strong, changing the very trajectory of your life. If we find ourselves pining for something, allowing it to consume us and drive us, this could be an indication that we have fallen out of balance in an area of our lives. Watch what you are striving for and work to keep your dreams, passions, and desires in check.

OUR FEARS

What scares you the most? What one thing would hurt you the most if you lost it? What strikes anxiety deep in your heart, so deeply that if it happened, you don't know how you would recover?

These are uncomfortable questions that strike at the heart of our self-sufficiency. They require raw, honest answers. These are questions that, if answered truthfully and with vulnerability, *will change your life*.

You see, you already know the answers to these questions. In your mind and in your heart you know what fears you have. You are familiar with the icy coldness of their fingers as they grip your heart in the quiet moments of life—the ones when the noise around you has stopped and the distractions faded away. You know each and every thing that triggers them—the headline news story, the conversation, or the circumstance that is out of your control. You know that no amount of denial can make these fears go away for long. They are always there, lurking just below the surface of your perfect life.

When I think of the many fears I've encountered over the years, I can see the ones I've broken free of. I can see the bondage I was in and how my automatic reactions were in many ways controlled by my fears. When I close my eyes to remember how I felt when I was controlled by fear, it's not a pretty picture.

For years, I had a strong fear of never measuring up, of being abandoned because I was not good enough. I remember this fear even as a child. If someone said something with disapproval, I would automatically shut down and introvert. I would pretend I was invisible and would stay invisible to the person I felt I had disappointed. Gradually, the fear of abandonment would pass by, and sometimes the person would never know they had been disapproving at all. My interpretation was what was real to me. I started to feel like an Egyptian mummy with this particular fear. I started covering who I was and what I thought. I would be silent if I disagreed with someone. I would make up stories in my mind, using the real life experiences of disapproval, and give them all happy endings, hoping that if I stayed invisible long enough my experience would have a happy ending as well.

I remember feeling completely paralyzed when I once disappointed my 3rd grade teacher by losing my notebook with my homework in it (we later found where I had inadvertently put it in the wrong cubbyhole). Even after the notebook was found, I had cried as I clutched it to me out of the fear that my teacher would no longer be nice to me. I sat quietly for at least a week, eyes downcast, trying again to just be invisible.

Obviously, that fear was deeply ingrained in me and it took several wake-up calls for me to understand that people weren't lurking around waiting to befriend me and then abandon me. Once I was on the other side of the fear, I was able to examine it and make sure it was put out to pasture for good. To be honest, I still feel it when I am overextended socially. After all, it was a strong pattern for years. But I can see it for what it is now, and when it comes calling, I know how to stop it. I am walking in freedom from that fear now and can use my negative memories of living with it to help me not give in to what was once a very familiar companion in my mind and my heart.

To me, that was what my fear looked like. For you, what does your fear look like? How has it impacted you as a child and now as an adult?

Take a moment to be vulnerable with yourself. *What fears have you battled in life? What fears have haunted you? If we were having a counseling session together, what stories would you tell me about that fear? Would it still grip you?*

Our fears come in many shapes and sizes. My fears may not match yours. I've studied my fears. I've analyzed them. And some of them have disappeared once I brought them into the light of day. Fear doesn't like light. Fear doesn't want to be talked about. It is a strong emotion tied to a strong belief that hovers in the dark recesses of our minds. It is stronger than anxiety. It is fueled by thoughts, teachings, experiences, and emotional ties. We become connected to the fear and it becomes intertwined with who we are. Often, we've lived so long with our fears that we use them as headlights to see what's coming our way and how to avoid or handle the potential problems we see. When we use our fear as a guiding light, it's easy to see how that could lead us astray and create some seriously adhered to patterns of belief and behavior.

We also use our fears to justify our actions. We use them to rationalize our choices and sometimes we use them to continue to give control away to other people. Anytime we introduce change in our lives, you can bet that fear won't be far behind.

Here are some common areas that fear runs rampant within us. If left unchecked, the consequences are detrimental to the overall quality of our lives.

- New opportunities

- Relationships
- Work
- Finances
- Goals

How does fear show up in these and other areas? What types of fear are there? Endless variations. Here are a few.

- Failure
- Loss
- Hurt/Pain
- Heartache
- Financial Hardship or Destitution
- Inadequacy
- Regret
- Boundaries
- Responsibility
- Abandonment
- Being taken advantage of
- Being wrong/incorrect
- Being empty
- Falling short
- Being challenged
- Losing independence
- Connecting
- Not knowing
- Looking bad
- Taking control

Some of our fears seem perfectly rational to us. They are worn like armor or a shield and wielded like a sword. We think they are protecting us. We think they are safe to keep around. The exact opposite is true.

If I had allowed my fear of abandonment to continue to rule my thoughts, how different would my life be? Only I know the vast difference in direction my life would have taken.

If there are any fears you used to have in your life that are no longer present, think about the ways you overcame that fear. Think of how different your life would be if you had not crossed the bridge to freedom and put each fear far behind you. Only you know what you would have missed out on had you not stood up to your fear.

Most likely there are still fears that are active in your life, as there are in mine. The human psyche is not one-dimensional. The bigger fears can surface first for those of us who are ready to be completely honest and vulnerable regarding this topic. The smaller fears may only come to mind for you now if you aren't ready to commit to full disclosure with yourself. We can start anywhere, with large fears or with small. Each time we conquer a fear, we will experience relief and freedom. But, the path won't be straight and predictable. For each person it will vary.

Once you rid yourself of the fears that came to your mind a few moments ago, you may think that's it and there is no more. Unfortunately, just as we aren't one-dimensional people, life isn't a dreamland. Circumstances will arise that, if we're not careful, allow new fears to take root. Or, as I've seen in my own life, the fears I didn't know I had or wasn't ready to recognize as fears will come to the surface when you least expect them to. Be patient with your humanness when this happens, but also be aggressive in labeling the fear and handling it.

Pep talks aren't the answer to deeply rooted fears. I've tried that approach with mostly a lack of success. We can only fool ourselves temporarily.

~§~
*If the fear has taken hold of me and been residing in my mind
and belief system for years, it is illogical to think that a series of
pep talks or motivational lectures will fix the problem.*
~§~

I do not believe that a pumping ourselves up emotionally is the answer to a deeper issue that needs sincere effort to overcome. There are a few temporary fixes that come to mind in the realm of trying to pretend our fears don't exist. Take a look at this list and see if you've tried any of these to compensate for a deeper fear that exists in your life.

- Financial success
- Educational achievements
- Social groups
- Sex
- Alcohol
- Binge eating
- Obsessively working out
- Motivational/Pep-talk materials
- Busyness
- False levity
- Our children and their schedules
- Hobbies
- Competition
- Community or other awards
- Volunteerism

The list is endless and as varied as we each are. Temporary fixes are just what they look like: a momentary relief of the underlying fear.

How can we truly conquer our fear? By taking logical action steps to correct the foundation that supports the fear. Somewhere along the line, we believed a lie about ourselves, our lives, or something that is deeply connected to the fear. Identify the lie and each time that fear arises in your mind, stop listening to it. You may have to intentionally stop listening to it 50 times a day at first. Eventually, the lie will lose its power if you show perseverance and fortitude. If you start the fight to end your fears and stop midway, you run a high risk of the fear coming back with even more strength and potency (I have seen this!). That is the power of our mind using an old pattern to comfort itself when new patterns haven't been reinforced long enough.

Once you stop the lie, you can begin to replace it with a short word or phrase that will help you to remember a truth associated with the fear. For my fear of abandonment, I had to tell myself I was wanted. That's all it took for me to eventually switch loyalties from the fear over to the truth. For you, it could be an entirely different truth. Usually people can think of a truth quickly, and our first instinct is typically the one to go with in cases like this. If we overthink it, we can end up writing an elaborate paragraph that we will never remember to say or have time in the moment to use to combat a fear-based lie. Keep it short and to the point. And be sure to remember to use it, no matter how frequently, each day.

Some examples of short, truthful words to replace lies of fear that have accumulated in your mind are:

- I am not worthless.
- You do not own/control me.
- My opinion has value
- My ideas are good.
- I do have a voice and will use it.
- I am okay without (insert person's name) in my life.
- You are my equal, not my superior.
- I am strong.
- (Insert name) has no right to control or manipulate me.

In the end, you will find that your fears aren't controlling you at all. Don't be discouraged. Freedom is waiting for you, and for me. We can do this.

OUR PEOPLE, OTHER PEOPLE

A couple went in for marriage counseling. The wife sat on one end of the couch. The husband sat at the other end. The husband looked slightly nervous, the counseling session not being his idea. The wife looked defiant and annoyed. She crossed her arms and pressed her lips firmly together in a prim line. Everything about her said she was the offended party and would not be moved in her opinion on the subject of their disagreement.

The counselor took a moment to survey the couple before starting the session. Then, the session began. Faster than any other couple, these two spilled out their issue within five minutes. It was obvious they both were desperate to fix the problem, but both of them had their own ideas about how to go about it.

The situation was fairly straightforward on the surface. The husband's father was older and not as mobile as he used to be. He lived less than ten miles from the couple's home. Recently, the father lost his wife and began to call his son (the husband) daily, asking for small favors such as running errands or driving him somewhere. At first the wife, in sympathy for his loss, said nothing about these daily requests, even pitching in to help. But over several months, she noticed that her father-in-law did not actually need the help he was requesting. He was capable of driving, and he had several long-term friends who lived close by. He was not hurting for companionship. She spoke to her husband about it and received no support from him. In her opinion, her husband was blinded by a sense of duty to his father to be there even if it meant cancelling or altering plans with her or their friends. As you can see, over time the issue became a huge point of contention for them. The wife lost respect for her husband as he repeatedly left dinner early to answer a call from his dad. She spoke to their grown kids about the situation, but received little understanding from them. After all, they were long gone and had lives of their own. A year after the passing of her father-in-law's wife, she stopped talking to her husband. That caught her husband's attention, and, after several failed attempts to finally resolve the problem themselves, they came into counseling.

From the wife's perspective, her husband's father was controlling and manipulating her husband. From the husband's perspective, he was paying his dad back for all the support he'd received from his parents as a child and while in college. For the couple, it looked like a dead end street with no way out of the anger and hostility that had accrued over a year's time. The counselor recommended what every good counselor recommends: baby steps. Make one small change a week, have third party accountability, and fight the old patterns when they arise.

For this couple, the husband became tired of hearing his wife 'nagging' him about his rudeness to her in dropping everything to go help his dad. As a result he stopped listening to her until she stopped talking and withdrew from him. That is a negative pattern. The wife tried to regain love and commitment from her husband by forcing him to see what she saw. She thought that by repeating her message to him, he would finally hear it and take action. Instead, he tuned her out and in anger. She then decided to give him a piece of his own medicine and tuned him out. That, also, is a negative pattern.

It took both of them two additional years to retrain their minds and regain control of the situation. The pushback from the husband's father was, as expected, heated and filled with manipulation.

One of the most unpleasant sources of control for us to explore usually is in the realm of family members or those very close to us. We don't like seeing 'our people' through the lens of reality. We don't like exploring the possibility that perhaps the people we care the most about could actually be manipulating us, controlling us, or violating our boundaries, as the husband's father did in our example. Any time we seek to make a change in a close relationship, the kick back from the other person hits closer to home than we would like to experience. Often, this leads us to avoid making any changes, even though it may be obvious that the person or people are indeed violating our boundaries.

This takes us back to the classic question most people ask me: how do I know for certain if the interactions with others and the behaviors of others are healthy or unhealthy for me?

The answer is directly contingent on how self-aware you are. If you have not yet taken the time to get control of your thoughts and feelings, the likelihood of you being able to accurately define healthy boundaries with others is very low, if not impossible. If, however, you have taken steps to monitor yourself and remove negativity from your life, you will be able to more easily see when someone is exerting undue power over you or trying to control you in ways that are not appropriate.

First you need to put boundaries firmly in place within your mind. Then you will need to monitor them. Once those are secure, turn your attention to others close to you. Here are some questions to ask yourself in regards to how others are interacting with you.

- Are people in your life saying or doing things that trigger you toward anger, shame, regret, or embarrassment? If so, are the comments intentional or accidental?
- When you spend time with someone in your family, do you feel better or worse from the experience afterwards?
- If you are expressing your opinion, your desires, your dreams, or your thoughts, do others cut you off or try to 'one up' you with a better idea or opinion? If they do, this is a sign of a boundary being crossed.
- Do people in your life constantly try to give to you only to then turn around and heap expectations on you?
- When you put effort into a family member, do they say things that make you feel guilty that you haven't done more for them or done something sooner?
- Are there people close to you who repeatedly ask for help or for favors where there is not sincere, legitimate need for the help or favor?

The list goes on, but these are a few basic identifiers to see if someone close to you is controlling you or manipulating you. If you have identified some manipulative people in your life, take a moment and envision the tug-of-war rope. How much of the rope have you given away to the other person or other people? Can you see how the steps unfolded for you to give that control away? Usually we don't give two feet away at one time. Generally, it is a gradual process of inches that may never stop until we either have no boundaries left or we decide stand up for ourselves.

Every person alive has motives for what they do or say. Human nature is simply that way. I've discovered that it is far easier to read the motives of someone who is not close to us rather than to accurately see the motives of someone we care about.

A friend of my family was the second eldest of four siblings. Every year at Christmas he amazed his sister and brothers by how accurate he was in knowing what their mom wanted for a present from them. I was rather impressed myself until at a social gathering his phone rang and he answered it. I thought that alone was odd, as the setting was not one where people were on their phones. He proceeded to carry on a conversation, and it soon became apparent that he was talking to his mom. Based on what I heard, I knew she was laying the foundation for a rather elaborate Christmas present that she wanted. In fact, she was clearly giving him two expensive options to pass along to her other children. Over the years, she must have discovered that he was the most prone to overlooking her manipulation and was willing to work his siblings to invest in presents she wanted. I'm not against people expressing what they would like to receive at Christmas, but I am very on guard when someone begins to drop hints and then cop an attitude if the hint isn't picked up and acted upon.

When he was off the phone, a few people close by said something to the effect of, 'Your mom's working you again this year, isn't she?' It was said in jest, but he became extremely defensive. He couldn't see what everyone else could see because he genuinely loved his mom and thought the best of her. I do not know if this situation ever resolved itself, but it saddens me to see people being controlled and totally oblivious to it.

It's not just parents, of course, who can control us. Siblings can as well, and even children can. Children who learn to control and manipulate when they are young, grow up to repeat patterns of control and develop expectations that are extremely unhealthy. I once saw a child ask his mom for something while at a grocery store. The mom said 'no' and continued down the aisle, looking for an item on her list. The little boy literally stopped, quickly analyzed the situation and realized that his mom was walking away from the item that he wanted. He acted fast by running to catch up to her, wrapping his arms around her legs, forcing her to stop, while grinning up at her and declaring how much he loved his mommy. The manipulation worked. The mom, feeling love for her child and oblivious to how she had just been controlled, gave the child what he wanted when he asked her again, still hugging her.

A basic rule to prevent manipulation is to first be careful when you say 'yes' or 'no', and second, if you have said 'no', make sure it remains a firm 'no'. Otherwise your child will learn your weaknesses and play to them in order to get what they want. It doesn't mean children are bad. It simply means that human nature dictates that unless we are trained, we will do what we need to do in order to get what we want, no matter our age.

The grocery store story doesn't actually end there. I saw the same mother and child in the check out line. He had already eaten whatever treat he had worked to get earlier and was asking for a sugary drink. This time the mom stood her ground and said 'no'. He tried one form of manipulation, the hugging technique, but it failed him. He then sat back in the seat of the cart and took a deep breath. He was gearing up to throw a loud fit. The mom looked annoyed and actually gave the child something to drink, though it wasn't the drink he wanted!

It doesn't mean the mom was a bad mom. She wanted her child to be happy. However, it is likely she may not have set ground rules for her child or taught him how to respect boundaries.

To you, it may not be obvious you're being manipulated, but to others it can be painfully obvious. If you are in doubt, seek a healthy, wise, mature outside opinion but be willing to listen to them if they start to tell you the hard truth you may not want to hear.

~§~
Ultimately, it is up to you how much manipulation you allow in your life.
~§~

Why do groups and clubs exist? Why do runners join or start a running group where participants get together and jog? Why do avid readers of particular genres join book clubs? Why do people who collect coins join a coin collecting association? Sometimes it can be for the camaraderie of being out around people. Most often, though, people join groups to be around like-minded people. When we join a club or group that is focused on our hobbies or passions, it bolsters our interest and supports our endeavor to continue the hobby. In short, the group influences us, our thinking, our perspective, and even the amount of time we put into our hobby.

A friend of mine is Canadian. A year ago, recently married, he was looking to improve in a certain aspect of his leadership skills. His wife was more assertive than he was at that time, and they both felt that he could use a bit more balance in this area. He and I began a community project together and I quickly saw what she meant. He had great ideas but was very slow to follow through, making him seem unreliable when he actually wasn't intending to be unreliable. He found an organization that offered a weekend conference for people who were at the same point he felt he was in his journey of growth as a leader. With great excitement, he signed up. His wife was cautiously optimistic as her husband's laid-back personality was affecting his job as well as their relationship.

My friend came back from that conference a new man. The people he met empathized with him, supported him as he supported them, and connected with him in ways people who are at a similar crossroads tend to do with each other. He felt validated and inspired. He wore his newly created 'life plan' like a badge, and stayed with the goals he set at the conference for an entire year. His wife was thrilled that her husband stopped withdrawing and began to connect with her, letting her in to his thoughts and being willing to stand his ground when they disagreed. His life was transformed, no doubt, but I was curious how he continued the momentum so long after leaving the conference.

What he told me opened my eyes anew to how powerful the

people we are around can be in our lives. While the conference was only for a weekend, and he had not traveled to any additional conferences since then, the vast number of people in attendance made it possible for local groups to form. He had several accountability partners he met with regularly in a small group forum, and the influence of the group on him was positive and long lasting.

By regularly attending the small group and giving some elements of control away to the group, my friend intentionally lowered his boundary for the sake of self-improvement. It would be difficult to benefit from a mentoring type of relationship if you never shared anything personal with the mentors you had. In this example, the impact of social groups on my friend was beneficial, and the releasing of his grip on the rope was done with thought and consideration; it was temporary and all involved understood the purpose of the lowering of my friend's boundaries.

It's not always this way. The influence of some groups can push us in negative directions, alter our thinking, and even change our behaviors. These influences are not always overt. The changes can happen slowly, over time. Each time we visit the group, new ways of thinking like the group are reinforced and rewarded. If, while you were reading this paragraph, a situation or group came to mind, it might be worth exploring to see how that group may be influencing you more profoundly than you realized. In fact, you may have inadvertently given a great deal of control away that now you will have to work diligently to take back.

~§~
We don't have to allow peer pressure, social pressure, or group pressure to alter who we are.
~§~

This truth includes our co-workers, our bosses, our teachers, our mentors, our friends, our religious leaders, our political leaders, and our community leaders. Listening to the wisdom of others can be a rewarding, positive experience. But blindly following others just because of their power or position is equivalent to holding your control in your hands and suddenly opening your hands to allow someone else to take all they want.

Just because a group is teaching a certain philosophy or engaging in activities you may not normally engage in, does not mean you need to go along or you have to go along. If you're feeling pressured, take a moment and reconsider how much control you are maintaining and how many of your personal boundaries are in place.

Here are a few ways that we can feel the group's energy pulling us:

- Their expectations
- Their perspectives
- Their goals
- Their energy
- Their beliefs
- Their words
- Their vision
- Their actions
- Their instructions

It's plausible that we may not be exactly where we want to be in these or other areas of our lives. There is a marked difference in recovery between giving a small amount of control away versus giving a lot of control away. What if we see areas in our life that for months or years we already have given a lot of our personal power away? How do we get that back?

As you ponder the areas where you may have let go of your boundaries, let's start looking at the different levels of control and what to do if control has already gone too far.

SECTION THREE

WHAT IF CONTROL HAS ALREADY GONE TOO FAR?

HOW DID WE GET HERE?

Have you ever watched a nest of ants build their home? Or a spider carefully and intricately weave its web? Or a bird faithfully construct its home of twigs, painstakingly choosing each piece before weaving it together? The end result is a combination of each step along the journey. The end result is a compilation of every choice made before.

If the bird has a bad day, is tired or moody, and decides to choose a twig that is fractured or too brittle, what will happen? The entire nest will be compromised. Maybe not by much, but enough to weaken the structure and put pressure on other pieces that may then eventually not withstand the weight of the eggs. If the bird is not diligent, the nest could easily fall apart in the wind and rain of the first storm. That would jeopardize the safety of all the eggs.

What about the ants? I've watched nature videos that show how complex an ant colony is. If one ant fails to do its job, the entire colony suffers. Why? Because each ant has a very specific role, and each role is critical to the good of the whole colony.

And we all know about spiders. We have seen them scurrying along to get out of sight, or hovering in dark corners. Have you ever seen them building a web? Each connecting point matters for the strength of the entire web.

At any point of these building processes, a poor decision can be made. Each poor decision affects the bigger picture in both small and large ways. It's the same for us. Every day, we are faced with hundreds of choices. And each of these choices carries with it a consequence – either for our good or our harm. Some of these consequences are life changing. Others are just the difference in nutrition between ordering a salad or a sandwich at lunch.

~§~
Every choice starts a series of events or continues a series of events.
~§~

For example, if you've had a string of bad days and you continue to view life through a skewed lens that says everything is hard, then the consequences are going to be that everything IS actually difficult. But if you choose to change one thought from a complaining thought to a positive—but still true—thought, then you have stopped, for the moment, the negative series of events. As you continue to make conscious choices to have positive thoughts, you will effectively be beginning a new series of events in your life. Our filters are so powerful they can be the difference between making a beneficial connection with someone, successfully interviewing for a job, turning a failing relationship around, or feeling so negative you don't even try for any of these things. Our thoughts define our lives.

When I'm consulting with groups of managers, I put it to them this way: Thoughts lead to feelings. Feelings lead to beliefs. Beliefs lead to attitudes. Attitudes lead to actions. Actions lead to reactions.

The beginning and most critical link in this chain is our thoughts. From these flow the rest of the links. If we see a problem with any of the links, you can be sure it can be traced back to our thoughts. For example, if we are exhibiting a poor attitude, we will be able to trace it back to a faulty belief. The issue with what we are believing can be traced back to how we feel about something. This, in turn is based on what we are thinking about that something. We can mask the truth of this for a while at any link, but sooner or later, we will need to go back to the beginning of the chain and correct the thoughts.

If you've ever weeded a garden you know that it's of little use to remove only the top part of the weed, the part that's showing. Within a short period of time, the weed will grow back and you'll have done little good. If you get to the root and remove the entire weed, then you will have made progress in your garden. Our minds are the same way. Changing behaviors or learning to mask our feelings or hide our true attitudes is not going to take us to a place of freedom. We must go deeper…back to the beginning thought behind the choice.

In what other ways do our choices affect us? They affect us when we allow others to start to take control of us. This can be any of the types of control we've already discussed, or this can be something more serious like abuse. Abuse comes in many shapes and sizes, but the most common seems to be emotional abuse. Physical abuse carries with it the marks of the event, but emotional abuse is the wearing down of someone's sense of self worth, self-respect, independence, and freedom to be an individual. Emotional abuse tells the abused that you have no choice and that you can't do anything without the abuser's permission or presence. These are serious topics, and there are a myriad of excellent resources available through an Internet search.

What I want to explore is the role our choices play in allowing others to control us. What are the steps of that process? What is our mental reasoning when we start to give control away? What if we have already given an enormous amount of ground away? What do we do now?

What I've discovered in my own life is this: my choices build upon each other to create a web of boundaries, beliefs, and allowances in my life.

We've already discussed boundaries. We know what beliefs are. What are allowances? I'm not talking the kind of financial aid that a child receives from a parent so they can go buy or do something they want. I'm talking about are the flexible lines we draw in our minds, not the boundary lines but the gray area that is not a solid 'yes' or a solid 'no'. It's tied to boundaries in some ways but the lines move around as life unfolds.

I'm a very scheduled person. I live by my schedules. If I say in my mind I will give 30 minutes to a person or project, then I will give only 30 minutes. If I plan my day with 15 errands in the day, then I hustle from errand to errand until I finish all of them. It doesn't matter to me if I'm hungry or see someone I know along the way. I stay focused and finish what I've said I'll finish.

I know a lot of people who aren't so structured. When they say they'll give half an hour to someone, they already know going into it that it may take longer than half an hour, so they make a mental allowance for the possibility of a change in plans. It may be that the conversation is so interesting that it requires more time, or it may be that the topics to be discussed take longer than anticipated. Instead of cutting off the meeting or pushing through the agenda consistently, they may allow the meeting to go much longer than anticipated. As a result, the rest of their day has to change because of this allowance they made. Some people have huge lists of things they will accomplish on a Saturday, their day of the week to run errands and finish home projects. They don't feel upset or like a failure if there are still half a dozen things left undone come Monday morning because they went into the weekend making mental allowances for what was most important and had to be done and what was not as important and didn't have to be done.

We do this every day. Allowances can be made for anything. If our child misses naptime and gets grumpy, we may make an allowance for his grumpiness because we couldn't get him home for a nap. If an unexpected expense comes up that breaks our budget, we may make an allowance for that because the expense was necessary, not frivolous. If our spouse is traveling and fails to check in to say that he or she landed at their destination safely, we may make an allowance for this because we know they are being met at the airport by their boss or contact person.

~§~
Allowances come in all shapes and sizes. Most often they are insignificant. Sometimes, they are vital.
~§~

What I've discovered is that allowances that are tied directly to our boundaries, our principles, or our beliefs, should not be altered very much or too quickly. If a spouse experiences one incident of emotional abuse and makes an allowance because the other person is under exorbitant amounts of stress, that is opening a new chain of events that could be detrimental to both parties involved. If an employee allows one inappropriate comment to hang in the air between them and a boss but makes an allowance for it because they are new to the company, that also is opening a door for a new type of 'normal' that is not okay. People are quick learners in some ways. They test others and figure out where their boundary lines are and how flexible they will be when push comes to shove. Many times, this is done without ever having a direct conversation about it.

By this point, you and I have already taken a look at our boundaries. We probably understand where our definite lines are, and what behaviors take us beyond where we want our boundaries to be. But what about the gray areas—the allowances? What about the areas that we haven't clearly defined or even thought about? Those areas are important to take a good look at and understand.

Initially, if someone violates a gray area, the response to the violator usually isn't that strong. After all, it's a gray area. If someone violates an area where circumstances are encouraging you to make an allowance, the same thing is usually true: you don't have strong reaction because of the allowance you're giving the person for the offense. What we don't often realize is that unexplored allowances actually create things like stress and psychological clutter in our lives. They also create a new type of normal, maybe not for us, but usually for the person we gave the allowance to. In our minds, the allowance may have been a one-time thing based on a certain situation, but in the mind of the other person, it created a new normal—a new standard for what is allowed—and a new string of events on their end given how they now look at us. This is one of the reasons maintaining boundaries and control is not often talked about. There are a million gray areas in the world.

My encouragement to you is to be aware of what allowances you have made or are making for others. How many excuses do you give to people? If you are the type of person to give a lot of allowances to others, take a moment and see how much accumulated stress and hurt feelings you are harboring. You may need to start today to reduce the amount of gray areas in your life, or simply begin to monitor those areas as well as your reaction to them.

If you made an allowance in an area where, at the time, it seemed like a wise choice to hold your peace rather than to speak out, but now you're having second thoughts, take a look at the situation with as much objectivity as you can. If you need to say something to clear the air or reestablish the authority of a boundary, proceed with wisdom (and the strength to see it through) to the appropriate end.

~§~
An allowance you may have given to someone may not be seen
as an allowance by that person. It may be seen as a norm that
was established between the two of you, or the group of you.
~§~

Making a change in this area is not easy because it involves other people. But if you take it one step at a time and stand firm when they push back, you can regain control of your boundaries and all the areas of allowance that you see in your life.

When we create a new *normal*, we are starting a new pattern. People are usually pattern-based. For example, we generally look for routines, we take the same route to work and go on autopilot, we buy the same foods from the grocery store, and we gravitate toward the same types of clothing or trendy fashions. We appreciate the comfort and simplicity of patterns.

Patterns are like every other neutral part of our lives. They can lose their neutrality when they become negative. What patterns in your life may be holding you back? What patterns of acceptable behavior may be clouding your vision for seeing the behavior for what it really is?

If you are entrenched in a long-term pattern of abuse, neglect, disrespect, or bullying, you will likely need outside help to monitor yourself as you walk out of the negative pattern. The first step is to actually see the pattern as something that is negative. Poor patterns are formed so quickly! A new, negative normal can take place within a week, and the past can seem like a year ago instead of a month ago.

Unfortunately, the time frame of forming a new pattern is not the same when trying to reverse the negative normal or poor pattern. Undoing the damage takes time away from the damaging party, and it takes repeated building up of the person who has been damaged. Often we are tempted to give up on ourselves or start to make even more allowances for the person who has hurt us or offended us. But it is worth the time and effort it takes to build a new pattern that will liberate you from the dark cloud and gain control of that area of your life.

Another way we allow negative patterns in our lives is simply by being too busy to examine our patterns and their effect on us. Countless times a week, we fail to take a look at our interactions or the way those interactions affect us because we are racing off to the next thing, the next goal, or the next interaction. Be careful that in your quest for goal accomplishment you aren't inadvertently giving ground away by being too busy to look at the allowances you are making and the patterns you are forming and reinforcing with others.

Sometimes we make allowances that we probably shouldn't, and we do this because we either have not been taught how to maintain good boundaries or we lack good, supportive influences in our lives. Think through who is influencing you and whether or not that influence is encouraging you toward healthy activities, thoughts, beliefs, and boundaries. If you have some negative influences in your life, remember that no matter how slight their presence seems to be, they can still negatively impact you. By limiting the amount of negativity in your life, you are helping yourself to walk in freedom and joy.

How well do you take care of yourself? Do you take care of your own needs or are you more concerned with the needs of others that you neglect yourself?

Another way we lose boundaries over time is because we are worn down. The more worn down we are, the more likely it is that we will make allowances that we would not normally make. Think of it this way, when are you most likely to binge eat or drink? When are you most likely to snap at someone instead of listening with your normal level of patience and empathy? When you're tired or worn out, right? We make excuses for our behavior when our energy levels are low. We may let ourselves off the hook because we want to avoid feeling deprived or because we worked really hard that day. We also make excuses for others' behaviors during those times, too, and we may not feel the energy to stand strong or push back when someone is testing a boundary. It's common, but it still can be kept in check. Look into this topic and how it relates to your life. You may need to reshuffle some of your priorities around to include prioritizing yourself!

We are what we think. Whatever we are putting into our minds does ultimately influence how we speak, act, and react. Monitor what is going into your mind and make a conscious choice of placing good and healthy things there. I remember reading a case study about the influence of visual media on our minds. They had a certain set of people watch primarily violent, bloody shows and movies. They had a second set of people watch primarily mild movies with happy endings. They then tested the stress levels of both groups, before and after. They also tested the levels of empathy in both sets of people, before and after watching the movies. What they found was most people had normal levels of stress and empathy before. But afterwards, those who watched the violent, graphic content had stress signals firing through their bodies at greatly elevated rates, along with significantly lower levels of empathy. The opposite was true for the second set of people who had not watched violence or gore. If anyone tells you that they are immune to being influenced by what they watch, know that they are simply fooling themselves. Plenty of studies show that there is a correlation between what we put in our minds and how we feel and act. If you want a more healthy life, try to be aware of what you let in your mind that may be influencing you in ways you don't want.

Another element of our minds is the types of things we think about. If we are constantly thinking worrisome thoughts, then it's plausible that our filter will be coated with anxiety and worry. If we think unkind thoughts about our spouse or coworker throughout the day, then it's plausible that when we actually see them and interact with them that our filter will be primed and ready to attack them or belittle them even before they've said a word to us. Be aware of the energy and nature of the thoughts you think!

A final way we can easily make allowances that aren't healthy for us is by zoning out and not engaging during decision-making moments or times of difficulty. When we zone out and don't deal with issues or actively engage in the choices we make, we are opening the door to a lot of ground being given over in the areas of control and boundaries. I know it can be easier at times to zone out instead of investing in the moment, especially if you feel it's not in your area of expertise, or if you sincerely don't care about the topic in the moment.

When I encounter clients who struggle with staying engaged, I don't advise them to leave our meeting and try to engage in every single thing that comes their way the rest of the week and beyond. I suggest selecting the top few things that are important and choosing to engage in those, gradually building their tolerance of engagement until it is more constant and less sporadic. Life is not meant to be lived by zoning out when times are tough or you are bored. But just as an endurance athlete has to gradually increase their tolerance for more distance, your mind needs an equally gradual and intentional increase in its tolerance for engaging with life.

If you sense you are off balance in any of these ways, start taking steps today to regain control.

LIVING IN AN UNSAFE ENVIRONMENT

In my early twenties, I taught a life-skills class at a group foster home for girls. I had several groups of girls come through my class over a three-year period. What struck me the most was how each young woman responded to kindness, love, and appropriate affection for that setting. Some of the girls completely shied away from any type of verbal affirmation, growing suspicious and distant. Other girls sincerely blossomed under the influence of honest compliments and words of praise. As I became familiar with some of them and how they came to be in this particular foster care facility, I heard stories of neglect, physical harm, drug abuse, and sexual assault from these young women. Not all of them came from the same backgrounds, but the ones who came from backgrounds where the environment was particularly restless, abusive, or unsafe exhibited a wide range of behaviors from being unusually defensive to overly submissive. They were directly influenced by the lack of security, positive communication, and unconditional love in their upbringing.

~§~
We all are impacted by the way we were raised. What we believe, how we interact with others, and how we respond to love or pain can many times be traced back to our formative years and the imprint the environment had on us.
~§~

If you've ever lived in an unsafe environment, you know the

uncertainty, chaos, fear, and stress that are involved. For some people, an unsafe environment means that the parent or spouse or roommate they are living with is emotionally unstable. For others, it means verbal abuse is happening. For still others, physical abuse and violence, or sexual abuse, may be occurring.

Some types of abuse require immediate outside help from professionals trained to assist people who are being physically or sexually abused. *If you are in that situation or have seen someone in that type of abusive situation the time to act is now. Immediately remove yourself or report abuse you have seen. There is no room for making excuses for a perpetrator who is physically or sexually harming someone.*

With verbal abuse, the damage is real and the after effects, long term. When we allow someone to verbally abuse us as adults, we often are responsible for allowing the boundary line to move in an unhealthy direction. If we were little children when this verbal abuse happened, or if this type of abuse began during a low spot in our lives when we were not healthy enough to stop it, it may be an instance where you are a true victim: the situation was out of your control and you were unable to stop it.

Fast forward many years after the verbal abuse has ended and what are you left with? If you have walked out of the situation or if it happened when you were a child and you grew up and left the situation as an adult, the sting, the damage, the patterns are still there unless you have dealt with them. The shame that usually builds inside of people who allow themselves to be verbally abused doesn't simply go away without putting effort into making it go away. The anger or the false strength or pride remains firmly in place unless we look beyond these latent defenses and see what is really going on.

What is verbal abuse or verbal bullying? It's very much what you would naturally think it is: anything that is said with the intention to hurt you, tear down your self image, control you, manipulate you, make you fight back verbally, cause you to feel stupid or inadequate.

When someone is on the receiving end of repeated verbal bullying, they will start to feel weighted down and negative about themselves. This occurs not only when they are around the person who is abusing them, but even when they are away from that person. The abusive words cause doubt, confusion, stress, and conflict within the person being abused.

A friend of mine had been verbally abused in her marriage. For four years she was repeatedly told that she was a bad person (in very specific terms), and each mistake she made—no matter how small— was amplified to such a degree that eventually her confidence was destroyed and the man she thought loved her became a monster in her eyes. Her children were young, she was a stay-at-home mom, her family lived across the country, and she felt trapped in an endless cycle of criticism and shame. She initially believed the comments and verbal invectives about how she was never measuring up, but over time the weight of his words shook something loose in her mind. Two things happened: she began to see the truth of who he was, and she also began to suffer from severe mental illness, battling bouts of depression and deeply rooted anxiety. As she walked away from him with her children, she faced a whole new set of battles as she struggled to walk through the fractures in her mind and become a whole person again with a healthy self-perception.

~§~
Verbal abuse is real. It is inappropriate and very damaging to those who are receiving it. Do not tolerate this or any other type of abuse in your life.
~§~

If you or someone you know is or has been verbally bullied, now is the time to take a stand and put a stop to this intolerable behavior.

There are other ways people can be abused as well, feeling trapped in a situation without power to easily escape it. One of these is emotional abuse from an emotionally unstable person. This type of abuse does not usually include verbal invectives or cruel tirades filled with anger and inflated egos. Emotional abuse can be subtle at first.

It can start with a favor, followed by another, followed by an expectation or a pattern that needs to be reinforced for you to think that you and the other person are 'okay'. If the pattern is broken, tears and drama follow suit, making you feel that you must continually help the other person just for them to get through the day. The motive behind the drama is the desire to control you.

I have known people who are inherently needy and actually enjoy this type of emotional co-dependency. The reason they enjoy it for a period of time is at first it seems to lift them up and fill them because they are not a whole person. The other party in the co-dependent relationship seems to shower them with attention and makes the needy person feel as though they can't survive without their friend. Meanwhile, during the time spent together or the time spent communicating, deep patterns of 'you owe me' are being built. If one person in this type of scenario decides to drop the ball and not perform to the expectations, things can become ugly very quickly. If the scenario were healthy, the other person would not be emotionally reactive and would let go as both people grew and changed. Insecure people easily get sucked into a variety of co-dependent, emotionally unstable friendships and relationships. These can escalate into emotional abuse, which causes innumerable problems and difficulties.

Emotionally unstable people tend to create an environment that feels unpredictable for those around them. They can resort to punishment methods when they don't get what they want. This type of punishment is different from the naturally occurring consequences of our poor choices. Usually, the methods of punishment are taken to an extreme. The motive is not to regain personal boundaries and control for them, but to hurt you and make you pay for whatever it is they feel you have done to not cater to them.

Some examples of punishment those who are emotionally unstable use include:

- Severely withdrawing love/affection

- Acting like they are the victim/manipulating your emotions
- Making you 'earn' physical intimacy by doing what they want
- Intentionally doing or saying things to cause pain/hurt
- Throwing a tantrum with excessive crying or wailing
- Making elaborate purchases that violate agreements you had previously made about budgets or long term financial plans
- Taking most or all of the money out of joint accounts
- Threatening to do things that would devastate the relationship and any remaining trust
- Talking about you behind your back and trying to incite others against you
- Attempting to destroy your credibility in your job or groups you belong to
- Taking items of sentimental value out of the house or out of your personal space and hiding or getting rid of them
- Threatening to take custody of the children or remove the children from the house
- Suddenly and drastically disappearing and refusing to answer calls or attempts to be in touch
- Calling or threatening to call the police to the house and claiming physical abuse or other forms of abuse

These are increasingly drastic measures that I have personally heard from people who are dealing with an emotionally abusive person. These forms of punishment are real and they create scars on those who endure this type of treatment.

Children who grow up with this type of controlling parent or guardian begin to believe that love is not a gift but rather an ever-changing series of rules and expectations that are difficult to understand and even more difficult to please. When someone comes along who offers them kindness without strings attached, they are suspicious and either withdraw or confront the seemingly 'too good to be true' offer of friendship and love. Multiply this suspicion times many years and you have an adult with deep wounds that need air, light, and space to heal.

I've known more than a few people who have had difficulty bonding with others, largely due to negative experiences they've had with either verbal or emotional abuse. The inherent trust that healthy families instill in each other was taken from many of these people and replaced with manipulation, meanness, and selfishness. The foundation many healthy adults enjoyed as a child is not always in place for people who come from a background filled with the difficulties outlined in this chapter.

Sometimes people can be raised in a fairly healthy household as a child, but then as an adult experience an abusive relationship. The ramifications are just as real for an adult who is walking out of abuse as it is for a child who lived the abuse during such a formative time.

Any one of us can be pulled into an unhealthy interaction with another person. No one is above temporarily losing site of appropriate boundaries. The important thing to remember is that immediate action and correction of a momentary lapse in personal boundaries is vital to your continued success walking in freedom and in control of your life. If you have been abused for any length of time, know there are resources available to support you and help you heal. Calling a help-line or looking on the Internet for this type of support is a real first step you can take to escape these bad situations.

~§~
The more we intentionally heal through receiving quality help, the longer lasting our recovery will be and the more clearly we will see the truth of our situation.
~§~

It's easy to kid ourselves or lose perspective on the affects of abuse. If we have a trained professional walking through the situation with us, we will have less opportunity to fall back into the poor patterns of the past.

We need people in our lives who will hold us accountable to live and walk in truth. Our minds are able to paint a memory or a picture of the past that is simply not true. If we begin to buy into these untruths, we will not truly heal from our experiences and will be more likely to fall into similar patterns again.

Learn from the past. Move on from the past. But do not allow a false or inaccurate perception of the past to take root in your mind. If you want to walk out from under the dark cloud I described in the beginning of this book, if you want to hold tightly to the tug of war rope, you will need to look at the pain and the trauma for what it is— not for what you wish it had been or what your emotions tell you it was. If you're struggling with this, seek professional help and know that your struggles are not unique. You are not weak, dumb, or deserving of punishment or shame. You are not alone. You are a fighter who chooses to take the path toward freedom, no matter how difficult. With the right support system you can make it through to the other side of each struggle a stronger, healthier, and more in control person than you were before.

WHAT DOES IT LOOK LIKE WHEN WE GIVE CONTROL AWAY?

Christie was a healthy, active young woman. Her mom was divorced with two physically disabled sons to care for. Both mother and daughter were similar: extraverted, busy, and joyful. Christie was attending community college and stopping by her mom's house a few weeknights every week. She would help with her younger brothers' care and spend time with her family. She had stable relationships with her friends, and had dreams of being a physical therapist one day. That was Christie before she met a new young man who was a coworker at a local restaurant. He became a friend, and eventually her boyfriend. At first, Christie's mom noticed that her normally happy daughter was becoming withdrawn and often looked deep in thought. She thought it was due to an upcoming decision about transferring from the community college to a state college, and did her best to give her daughter extra time to get her studies done.

Over a period of months, Christie gradually stopped coming over to her mom's house. She, a natural beauty with strawberry blonde hair and a carefree style, dyed her hair the darkest shade of indigo imaginable and began to wear an excess of makeup. Her mom hoped her daughter was just trying to find her way to adulthood and said nothing about the new look. Her mom did mention that she missed seeing Christie, and her daughter's response was the first indication that something was wrong. Christie became hysterical and defensive, crying and raising her voice about being old enough to have her own life without being told what to do. Her mom, already overwhelmed with the care of her two sons, withdrew emotionally and pushed aside her daughter's overreaction for the sake of peace.

Christie's mom had found a new school for her youngest brother that could better cater to his needs. Christie agreed to come by and support her brother during this transition on his first day. When he cried that he couldn't go to his old school anymore, Christie bawled along with him, and looked embarrassed for doing so afterward. Christie began to do many things that were erratic, forgetful, and quite unlike her. Those around her wondered what new pressures in her life were causing such apathy, bouts of annoyance, and constant fatigue. It was some time later that her mom found out there was a new boyfriend in Christie's life. The boyfriend had gradually worked his way into Christie's life until, in her mind, she felt she couldn't go anywhere or do anything without either asking him or bringing him along. She knew she was giving control away initially, but the new normal became reinforced with each step toward dependence she took

The unexplained detachment from people she was once close to, the extreme defensiveness when her mom expressed missing Christie, the undue emotionality, the forgetfulness and apathy, and the sudden and drastic changes in her appearance were all clues that something was deeply bothering the young woman. When her mom discovered her daughter had dropped out of college without telling her, she decided on an intervention. The boyfriend wasn't supposed to be there or know about the meeting. But, like many who are emotionally abusive and controlling, he found out about the intervention and showed up a few minutes after everyone else did. You can imagine the rest. Christie was so far along the path toward giving up control of her life to her boyfriend that the intervention did not help.

Often when we are starting off down the path toward giving our personal control away, we will display vivid signs that we are in the midst of an unpleasant or unwanted transition. Even if we haven't yet identified in what ways we are giving control away, our brains know that something is wrong. It's as if we are trying to protect ourselves from danger by sending up a signal flare for help. Once we have succumbed to the controller, bully, or abuser, we can sometimes find a middle ground of acceptance in our minds. Our normal shifts from healthy boundaries to justification of the person bullying us.

That's what Christie did. In her mind, she couldn't allow the thought that her boyfriend was in the wrong. Initially she knew he was, but repeated violation of her healthy boundaries resulted in a vibrant young person being shut down, confused, isolated, and in pain. Eventually, he crossed too many lines and she was forced to face the truth. He left her, took her savings, and was gone from her life without much warning. At that wake up call, Christie had to start seeing him with a clean filter. When she did, the thought that she had given so much of her life away to someone who was abusive crushed her anew. Thankfully, her mom and brothers were there to support her transition back to a firm foundation.

Symptoms of losing boundaries and giving control away can show up at work, too.

A few years ago I watched a documentary that outlined the difference between being the 'boss' in a company versus being an employee. The camera crew followed two bosses around for a few weeks and then followed two employees around for a few weeks. What came out of the documentary was astonishing. Those who felt they were in control of their job behaved differently on camera than those who felt that their job was in some ways, out of control. One of the employees spoke to the camera stating that he had constant anxiety, felt depressed, and was prone to bouts of unexplained emotionality. He suffered from irregular eating patterns and habits (sometimes going without food or sometimes gorging), as well as chronic fatigue and lack of sleep. He claimed his problem was someone at work who, instead of answering his questions and supporting his efforts, would speak negatively to him and about him. This type of public bullying and ridicule broke down his sense of self worth to the point where going to work was difficult and sincerely painful to him.

Fast-forward a few months, and this same employee was in a different job with a different boss. He was performing up to standards, and was healthy and fit. Only two changes had occurred. First, he finally had enough of being bullied and had decided to seek a new position where the environment was more positive. And secondly, he chose a position that gave him tasks he felt confident in performing. The happy people in the documentary were already in positions that supported their areas of strength and gave them the feeling of control that they needed to have a healthy self-perception. This employee needed to initiate a life change in order to regain the healthy mentality and sense of personal control he once had.

~§~
We can't always initiate or control when life changes come.
~§~

A great many of us go through several life changes as we age, mature, and make new lifestyle choices. If you see signs in yourself or others who are close to you that indicate the person is struggling with a change or a current situation, please take the time to talk with them. Taking action early is helpful when it comes to people giving control away. When new patterns that are unhealthy become reinforced over time and morph into the expected norm, it is more challenging to break than when new patterns are just developing.

Here are some emotional changes or outbursts that can be red-alerts for us when we, or people we know, are going through a life change:

- Abnormal or extended apathy
- Irritability
- Anxiety (prolonged or unexplained)
- Mental confusion
- Disorganized thoughts
- Depression
- Easily angered
- Restless behaviors or attitudes
- Unwarranted guilt or shame
- Resentment
- Hyperactivity or hyper thoughts
- Scattered attention
- Unusual splurges (financial, food, and other binges)

Often, we think young adults or children are the most impressionable. The truth is, we all are impressionable to varying degrees throughout our lives. Whatever your level of impressionability is when life is going well, multiply that many times over again and that's usually how malleable you will be when you are facing a life change.

Think of entering a new company and figuring out what the pecking order, hierarchy, and various social groups within the company are. Or think of when you went to college or grad school and the challenges of finding people who were like you on campus. Think of meeting a new set of friends in a new city and being asked to go out the night before a big, important business meeting the next morning. Each of these scenarios comes with a scale of impressionability. Your better judgment may say one thing, but the lifestyles or priorities around you may impress themselves upon you, causing you to do something completely different. When you are in your normal routine, you may find it easier to make a logical, rational decision. But when in the midst of a life change that has forced you out of your routine, you may find it harder to stop entertaining those ideas in your mind that lead to emotional choices rather than logical choices.

Each time I have moved from one state to another, or one city to another, the situation has brought change to my life. Not too long ago, I helped a family move from one end of town to a neighboring village. Their old neighbors had routinely watched the kids and loaned the family tools and supplies when needed. The family publicly thanked these neighbors for their generosity and expressed how nice it was to have them as 'family'. The new neighbors set a different standard from the beginning: you're on your own. They set boundaries around their space, and gave everyone around them ample personal space as well. My friends discussed this difference, and in the midst of the changes of moving their family, concluded that it was 'normal' to keep your distance from neighbors and doubted why they had allowed their former neighbors to become so close. Prior to the move, it had seemed healthy to give and take from neighbors. Within the new environment, with emotions running faster than usual, their new neighbors impressed upon them that the old pattern was not healthy or acceptable.

Whether the old or new pattern was the better choice is a personal decision. The point is, the changes in their lives left them more impressionable than normal (though if you were to ask them if this was the case they would have vigorously denied it). We really don't see ourselves quite as clearly as we think we do.

How strong is our self-perception? How ingrained is the way we view ourselves? And, most importantly, if our perception of who we are and our value is changeable, how can we prevent ourselves from letting this control us?

I used to think my self-perception was strong. I used to think I wouldn't doubt who I was or where I was going. I think many of us go through that phase in our twenties.

~§~
At some point along the way we start to see that who we think we
are isn't someone who is invincible, like we've been telling ourselves.
Who we actually are is far more fragile than we care to admit.
~§~

In moments of success, excitement, or focus, our self-perception can be firmly in place. In those moments, we really do see ourselves as a giant who is marching forth toward victory, or a pillar of wisdom and strength who stands strong in times of adversity. In moments of failure, though, how do we see ourselves? In moments of pressure, how do we change? When we start to give control away to outside factors and other people, we in turn allow them to alter our self-perception. If we allow them to alter our self-perception, it's our responsibility to get that boundary line back in place.

From time to time, people will come into your life and speak truth to you. The truth they speak can hurt, but it allows us to see ourselves more clearly. Such events are not a negative altering of our self-perception, like the examples we just discussed. These are learning moments of growth. Usually, healthy changes in our perception of who we are do not result in feelings of prolonged shame or embarrassment or guilt. When a word of truth is spoken appropriately and these feelings occur they are short and do not linger.

Think of it this way. If you announce to a group of friends that you intend to get in better shape and build more muscle tone, would you be offended if the next evening one of your closest, most trusted friends gently questioned your ordering a calorie-rich meal and sugary dessert? If you could tell that your friend meant well and is trying to keep the question lighthearted so you reach your goals, you would likely be thankful they reminded you to stay focused on the bigger picture. Initially, you may be embarrassed or irritated that the meal and dessert you want to order isn't what you should order. But after a few minutes, you would probably be glad to rethink your meal plan and order something in line with your goal.

When it comes to your boundaries, being able to tell where someone is coming from and recognizing if it's a case of you making an allowance you ought not make, or them crossing a line they ought not cross is a huge part of maintaining proper control of your relationships, your self-talk, your perception, and ultimately your life.

SECOND CHANCES

We all know that giving someone a second chance can be an important part of building a relationship or helping them believe in themselves enough to continue trying. If we think back to the times we were given a second chance, we can probably see how it affected us. For me, second chances are easy to give when the offense is small. But when the offense is larger, it becomes more challenging.

I drive a lot for my work. Most of the time, I meet with my clients at their office. Recently, I was driving on the interstate and someone merged poorly and cut me off. I didn't think too much about it and continued on my way. About twenty minutes down the road we entered a construction zone and two lanes were shut off. I see a familiar looking car trying to merge into the remaining open lane, right in front of me. Sure enough, it was the person who had cut me off before, the one *not* on my list of favorite drivers! I admit, I wasn't exactly feeling like letting them come into my lane in front of me. But, I relented and I waved the person over.

The interesting part is, I told this story to a friend of mine who claims to have a huge problem with road rage (little things like an incorrect merge onto the highway really make him mad). Sure enough, to him, the incident was a big deal, and he would never have allowed the person to cut in front of him a second time. From my perspective, it was a minor infraction on the scale of proper road etiquette. To him, it was a huge deal. Our filters were different, therefore what we thought to be an appropriate reaction were worlds apart.

~§~
Second chances are important, but it's difficult to give someone a second chance when our filter tells us that the offense is huge.
~§~

Why was the infraction from the above example such a big deal for my friend but not for me? A few reasons are involved. First, my friend had a trigger that was already active and sensitive to the topic. A small nudge and his trigger flared up as if the nudge had been a smack instead. Second, my friend's perspective was off balance due to the emotions attached to the topic of our conversation. For me, to be cut off in traffic usually isn't a bother. I don't have that particular trigger (though I have other triggers). My filter's sensitivity on this subject is more in the middle of the scale rather than an extreme edge of the scale. I'm not overly reactive but I'm also not completely apathetic or in denial of my feelings.

When it comes to giving someone another chance, it's kind of like our example. We have to identify where we are on the scale of reactivity and sensitivity to know if we are healthy enough to give someone a second chance. If your boundaries have already been so completely violated that everything the person or group does causes you intense annoyance, chances are you will not be in a place to offer them a second chance, even if they desire it and are willing to amend their behaviors. And second chances are all about reconnecting.

The first part of reconnecting with a controlling person who has changed their ways is to both know where you are and to respect where you are on the path of reconciliation. Old, negative patterns do not get put to rest as easily as we would like. Even if the other person has made noticeable and measurable changes, we can still stop the healing process by our own words, actions, and reactions.

How is this possible? In three ways. First, we can fail to appreciate and praise the person's true changes. Next, we can target in on all the ways they are still not the person we would like for them to be. And finally, by bringing up past hurts and offenses when it's not necessary to do so.

It's not an easy task to reconnect with someone and give them a second chance when the wounds are still fresh and active in our heart. If you start reintegrating people who have hurt or controlled you into your life before you are ready to calmly hold your boundaries and let go of the past, you can actually make the entire situation worse. Bouts of anger, fear, crying, and indignation will come as the person does their best to walk out of their controlling tendencies with you but occasionally slips up. When you look at the person who has bullied or controlled you, sometimes all you will see is the damage they have done and all you will feel are negative feelings toward them. Rarely does the past completely disappear in our minds when we have been violated.

Also, if you start to feel safe and let your guard down, the slightest infraction from the other person can send you back a few steps in your recovery. That said, second chances are powerful opportunities to deepen our own character as we offer someone who has hurt us the chance to rebuild the relationship and the necessary opportunity to potentially hurt us again.

How can you know when you are ready to begin walking down the path of healing with the person who has hurt you? If both parties are willing to begin to change and respect each other, you have the first step well under way on your path back to a healthy connection. How fast should you go in the process? Seeking counsel is your best bet to pacing yourself. How do you know if you are ready to handle it? Making sure you are back in the drivers' seat of your emotions will enable you to stop reacting negatively based on your feelings and start exerting your will and mental power to overcome those inevitable emotions in the moment.

While road rage isn't a trigger for me, I do have other triggers that make it hard for me to give someone a second chance. When I'm working with a client, I plan out our schedule for weeks or months in advance. The services I offer require reinforcement, and if too much time elapses between sessions, people don't progress as quickly as they are capable of.

In the beginning when I was first starting out, I didn't always reinforce the need for timely appointments the way that I should have. I was flexible to offer a 'custom' approach to what people needed, including their scheduling times. Because I wasn't as stringent in reinforcing a fixed schedule, it became a trigger for me when someone would try to juggle the schedule last minute or drag out the sessions instead of staying with the original agreed upon plan.

The first infraction wasn't usually a huge deal back then. But by the third or fourth time, I was more than a little annoyed. I didn't outwardly react, and because I never worked through the issue in my mind, the trigger was born. For awhile when someone would change a date (before I changed my policy), instead of reacting in my mind at a level .05 I jumped all the way to a 4 or 6 on the annoyance scale of 1-10. I allowed the trigger to control me. I allowed the trigger I had created to dictate my reactions. Ultimately, I stopped giving people a second chance in this area. It took me rethinking my policy and creating a boundary I was comfortable with for me to resolve the trigger issue and find balance in this area. It still is annoying when people are routinely late or when people seem to disrespect my time with last minute changes or postponements, but the annoyance is back down under a 1 where it should be.

Triggers can prevent us from being free to give others a second chance. Watch out for anything that causes you to overreact, and get control of those things. If you don't control your reactions and triggers, *they will control you.*

~§~
A key to keeping your reactions clean and healthy is knowing how your filters are performing.
~§~

We all understand that air conditioning units use filters to keep the larger particles of dust out of our air vents. We don't want dirty air to circulate in our homes so we regularly clean or replace our filters. If we don't keep our filters clean, what happens? Everything in our homes, including us, is affected negatively. We may have an allergic reaction. We may see particles of dust floating in the air. We may have a dusty environment. Our visitors may become uncomfortable. Anytime we make a choice, remember, there is a consequence, a result, or a change in what happens around us. Each choice holds power. The movie *The Curious Case of Benjamin Button*, explains this in detail. The main female character would not have been injured for life had she made one small choice differently. The choice was an innocent one, but the point is incredibly well made.

Sometimes we wake up to a huge problem and we wonder how we reached that place. How did we suddenly become trapped? How did we out of the blue have a series of arguments with our spouse? How did we go from a healthy interaction with our boss to feeling afraid or angry? These changes aren't 'sudden' or 'out of the blue'. They happen based on our choices.

~§~
Don't ever forget this valuable truth: each thing we do, or allow, or encourage, or ignore will have an affect on us.
~§~

What else affects our filters? Regulation of our environment. We can take action steps to help our filters stay clean that don't directly involve the filter itself. Just as we dust our furniture, vacuum our floors, and use screens on our windows and doors to eliminate things that contaminate our air filter, we can regulate our surroundings to ensure our filters aren't being unnecessarily influenced in a negative way.

This is important. We need to be in control of our environment in a healthy way by keeping it clean. A dirty environment causes our filters to clog much faster than if we kept our environment clean. Most people who are responsible for cleaning their home know that waiting a month to dust everything is not the best approach. It takes much longer to remove the built-up layers of dust, and it's not pleasant to live in a dirty environment in the meantime. A better approach is to go over things bit by bit, monitoring them and seeing which spots tend to collect dirt faster. It's the same for life. Some areas of our lives will accumulate dirt on our filter faster than other areas. Know your surroundings. Know where you need to monitor more and where you can monitor less. Keep on top of your filter's health by staying engaged with your surroundings.

We don't always clean our homes by ourselves, though, do we? In families, we can divvy up the chores so each person does something and makes the responsibilities lighter. Or we can hire someone to do the work for us. Either way, we are relying on someone else to help us keep our house filters clean.

To help us keep our mental filters clean, we subconsciously rely on others, perhaps more than we think or more than we ought to. I believe in having accountability or help during times of difficulty. But ultimately, I believe we should take action steps to stay in control of our own lives. If you sense you are excessively relying on someone else as a sounding board, a support system, or a reassurance partner, now is the time to take action to create a healthy boundary.

I once knew a man who was physically strong, educated, tall, and a hard worker. He was kind to others and very positive. In short, he did not seem like the needy type. I can't recall ever having more than an introductory conversation with the man, as our roles in our group were very different. However, over time, I started to see a pattern with him, a pattern I do not think he was aware of. Though he initially came across as a strong member of the group, a leader in the management team, and an independent thinker, as he became more comfortable in the group, I saw something else. There were two people he actually looked to as a support system in ways that were too excessive to be healthy. He had little in common with these two, but age. I noticed that when he boldly announced his thoughts, they weren't actually his thoughts. They were mirror images of what the other two managers thought and wanted. I saw this pattern grow over time and the co-dependence become clearer.

What I started to wonder with this man was how this pattern began. What had happened that had bonded these particular colleagues together into such an unusual alliance? It was not long before I discovered the answer. The other two had been there for him after he had ended a relationship that was important to him. He had withdrawn, and they had happened to be nearby in the break room when he had an emotional moment of pain. That one moment opened the door to a potentially healthy bonding for the three of them. But it did not go that way. Instead, a pattern of co-dependence developed that was not beneficial for anyone involved.

When you are so deeply entrenched in an unhealthy reliance on someone else, it takes more than a snap of the fingers to get you back on track to healthy independence. I imagine if anyone were to approach this man and try to help him see that his dependence on the other two people was off balance, he would become defensive and slip into denial. Usually, it takes a large encroachment on a remaining boundary or a sudden change in the behavior of the co-dependent party to see that you have lost perspective on what a healthy level of reliance is versus an unhealthy level.

Some of us tend toward independence and relying on ourselves more easily than others. And this tendency can cause problems as well. For me, I've been told that my desire to remain detached can feel like a brick wall coated in ice. My tendency is to not discuss my pain or my issues, and to simply withdraw and work on things by myself. This is great in theory (from my perspective) because it allows me to at least attempt to fix something without bringing others into my problems. The drawback, from others' perspectives, is that I'm shutting them out. I'm not allowing them to see me as anything other than who I am when I think I've fixed a problem or my unhealthy tendency. I've learned and am still learning to find middle ground in this area. I don't want to look bad in front of others, and that is a huge motivator for me to isolate and fix things in solitude. For me, the battle is relying on others rather than just becoming rigid and not allowing anyone to help me.

Wherever you fall on the scale of this topic, do yourself a huge favor: find a balance between your neediness of others and too much independence from them. If you try to isolate, you may start to feel your heart growing a little smaller every week. If you try to draw others into your problems more than you should, you may start to feel worn out or over extended by all the obligations you have created. Neither extreme is healthy or attractive in someone.

Our filters are important to help us give appropriate second chances. Our level of reliance on others is also important to help us know when we are in or out of balance. Clean your filters and keep your balance.

SECTION FOUR
HANDS ON THE WHEEL

MAKING PERSONAL CONTROL A LIFESTYLE

Learning a new skill like riding a bike is not initially easy. You may fall off a few times or forget to use your brakes and run into something. You may swerve or lose your balance. You may scrape your knee and not want to get back on and try again.

A friend of mine has two granddaughters. The youngest granddaughter is four years old. He decided it was time to teach her how to roller skate. She was ecstatic to be able to go to the roller skating rink with her grandfather and learn how to skate. She chattered happily all the way there and when her skates were on, she stood up with glee and promptly lost her balance. Her grandfather caught her in time to keep her from falling. In that moment, she realized that skating was a lot different from walking. For half an hour, they carefully went around the rink, her grandfather catching her before she could fall. Eventually, though, she fell. Instead of giving up, she got back up and tried again. Little by little her grandfather backed away and let her find her way forward on her own. Without his initial support she probably would never have made it, but with his help, she was held in a safety net until she was ready to strike out on her own. My friend loves his granddaughter, and he relayed how he winced each time that she fell and how he wanted to just hold her up by her arms and not allow her to fall. But he couldn't do that. He had to let her try and learn how to skate.

As you journey forward, you may seek professional help to keep you accountable and to help you understand what appropriate boundaries look like in the areas you have given control away. Initially, you may need a large safety net—a firm hand holding you up—like my friend's granddaughter did. But as time goes on and you learn new skills, that same safety net can become a trap, holding you back instead of allowing you to move on. Each of us progresses at a different pace, so I can't tell you how quickly you will recover from whatever ground you may have given away. A lot of our recovery time has to do with our will. How stubborn will we be in reclaiming our lives? How firmly will we stand in the new truths we have learned?

When I was in my early twenties I wanted to learn to speak French. I had heard someone speak the language and I thought it was beautiful. I really wanted to expand my horizons and learn something new. I bought books and resources, I signed up for classes, I checked out videos from the library that were in French with English subtitles, and I had dreams of speaking French fluently. I was prepared to learn. I was prepared to grow. At least, I thought that I was. Once I was in the middle of my class, I realized how hard it was to learn a new language as an adult with a busy life. I realized how many times I would forget a word or phrase, or my pronunciation would be off. I awoke to the amount of time I would have to spend training my mind to think and speak in a way that was completely different than what I was used to. None of my friends could speak French. In order to not lose the knowledge I had started to accumulate, I needed to find people who were on a similar path as me, or people who were already where I wanted to be. The more I stayed on the path, the faster my progression was. Life moves at a rapid pace, though, doesn't it? Summers brought vacations with my family and then I moved. The next thing I knew, I had put my desire to learn off to the side, and with it, I had lost a lot of the knowledge and new patterns in my mind. When I tried to go back to it, I remember sitting with my old French book and not even remembering many of the basic words I used to know so well.

I am sure if we all think hard enough we can see times in our lives when we did what I did with my French lessons. We see an area in our life that we want to change. We prepare for the change, and may even start to change, but as time goes on we lose focus or we forget the importance of making the change at all.

Three main stopping points come to mind when I think of life changes and the challenges inherent to them. Other stopping points exist, but these seem to be the most prevalent.

~§~
Some of us may do the prep work but never take the first step.
~§~

Sarah was famous for starting things, generating ideas, and getting others excited about it. But in the end, she never quite did anything tangible about them. When I say she was famous, I mean everyone who knew her would tease her about her lack of follow through. Underneath the teasing was a lot of truth: she started with an idea, did some research, but never could quite take action and make the plan reality. She came to me when things were really bad. Her relationships, her job, her coworkers, and her level of happiness—all of these areas were suffering because of her lack of taking action steps. As we talked through some of the ideas she had formulated in her mind the prior few months, we both started to see a pattern and began to understand why she was not taking action steps.

Underneath our patterns are reasons, reasoning, and often justification. Her pattern was being the idea smith, the dreamer, and the enthusiastic one who could brainstorm great ideas. But when it came time to do the work or make the ideas happen, she was often the last one to a meeting or the first one to find flaws with the idea she had created the day before.

When we explored what was holding her back from taking an action step, we found pools of anxiety surrounded by the fear that all the people who were so excited about her ideas would stop praising her if the ideas failed. To her, losing the good will of those around her was a controlling fear in her life. When she dug a little deeper, she could see the many times she had withdrawn from a group or stopped contributing to a project because the energy of the team seemed to decrease or people temporarily experienced stress or lack of harmony. She internalized this and went into self-protect mode.

Maybe your pattern looks similar to hers, but your reasons are different. Some of the reasons we may never take that first step could include:

- Fear of failure
- Projecting a negative outcome
- Seeing the work involved
- Intimidation by the reactions of others
- Fear of losing friendships or relationships
- Not understanding the importance of the task
- Feeling overwhelmed
- Not having a strong will
- Being led astray by the words and influence of others
- Sitting in denial of the problems
- Not wanting to commit to any stance or plan

If you see a pattern in your life of having good intentions to do something but not quite taking an action step toward it, you may want to take a moment and reflect on your own personal 'why' behind the behavior. We'll never reach our finish lines in life if we talk ourselves out of taking the first step.

~§~
Some of us may start strong but never finish.
~§~

Imagine watching an Olympic runner representing your country. This person has trained and prepared for a long time. They can see the finish line in their mind. They know that the skills they have accumulated are strong and well practiced. You watch them get into their spot. You watch them take off. With speed they zoom ahead. It looks like they're going to make it in good time. But suddenly, they stop. They're not injured. They haven't lost any of their skills. They still know how to run with endurance. But it seems they've lost interest. Whatever the reason, they simply stop trying, and slow to a standstill. After a moment to slow their heart, they walk off the track and for the rest of their lives they hide away from the race and pretend that they didn't do all the training and prep work. They pretend that they hadn't once been on a beeline to finishing well.

That wouldn't happen would it? An Olympic athlete is hungry for the finish line. They have so thoroughly trained their mind to continue on to the end that the thought of quitting isn't on their radar. Their ability to focus is amazing. Their ability to remember their goals and keep their priorities in line is astounding. It didn't happen overnight, though.

Any one of us can train our mind to make small sacrifices each day for the sake of our goals. We live in a time where instant gratification is more prevalent than ever before. But if we want to regain our boundaries, we will need to start to put off what we want now for what we want overall in our lives.

I'm not saying distractions are always easy to push away. I'm also not saying that the journey toward becoming healthy is paved with roses and daffodils. But I am saying, when you are halfway down the path and you feel like you want to start replacing your priorities of self-healing and freedom with other things, you may want to pause and remind yourself of the importance you used to put on the goal you are working toward. Let's not allow distractions, diversions, other people, our own impulses, or anything to stop us from continuing the journey.

~§~
Some of us may get almost to the end but then quit.
~§~

This possibility is the saddest to see. When someone is so close to the end, but can't quite close the door to their unhealthy past, it's hard to not intervene and try to close it for them. Why would someone quit when they are on the last part of their journey? After standing their ground and applying new lessons, why would someone give up with freedom clearly in sight? A few reasons come to mind, all surrounded by one word: weariness.

As the hurdles we have jumped over to become healthy seem to accumulate in our mind, the last few can seem too high to handle. We may not have let go of some of our earlier hurdles, and the stress of change starts closing in around us. Or, we may just be worn down by the opposition we have in our lives or the external stressors that are unrelated to our course of change.

Have you heard the saying 'the straw that broke the camel's back'? That's how it can feel for us if we have been living in a very abusive or unhealthy relationship and are trying to get out and make significant changes. We stand strong on our path for a long time, but then we start to feel tired. We start to doubt if it's worth it after all. It's in those moments you may need a temporary safety net back in your life. Someone who can objectively help you remember why you are on the path and encourage you to finish well.

If you feel weary of the journey, know that you are not alone. A great many of us become tired of moving toward change. We may complain to ourselves that nothing we do is good enough. Or ask ourselves questions like, 'Why bother trying any longer? Where I am is good enough.' Or say things like, 'It's just not working anymore.'

Lots of these types of thoughts can take root in our minds. And in the moment they seem believable and even realistic. But they take us farther away from our goals rather than ushering us into that place of freedom. Be vigilant to what your needs are as you near the end of the path of regaining control of areas of your life. It's okay to seek new help or additional help at this stage. It's okay to share the feelings of your burden with the purpose of staying strong and seeing things through to the end.

Even after we successfully remove ourselves from an unsafe or unhealthy interaction with someone, the temptation can be to allow old patterns back in. This is normal. It's normal to think you're strong, but then to run into someone from the past who doesn't know all the work you've put into making healthy changes. They may interact with you in ways you just worked hard to walk away from. They may have expectations of you that are not relevant to you anymore. They may make comments that tear you down. Things like this can throw you off and leave you feeling confused or uncertain. Things like this most likely will happen in one form or another. Not everyone will understand the depth of your need to make the change, and as such they may not respect the changes you've made.

Self-doubt may creep into your mind. Anxious thoughts may try to erupt. Feelings of emptiness or sadness may try to gain access in your heart. Big changes create big reactions, some internal and some external. Little changes still create reactions, especially if there are many little changes happening at once. Simply knowing that this is normal and could happen will help you to remain calm and in control, no matter what thoughts or people come across your path. Keep your eye on the reason you started the journey in the first place. Remember your priorities and do your best to keep self-doubt and all the other negative thoughts and feelings at bay.

Know your patterns, accept them as being normal, and continue to create a healthy lifestyle, one choice at a time.

THE REWARDS OF LIVING A HEALTHY LIFE

Many psychologists believe our world is becoming increasingly egotistical and self-centered. With the popularity of social media and everyone sharing the details of their lives online with others, it is easy to lose perspective of one's image compared to the reality—*what I am versus what I project*. But this increased focus on our image has a positive upside that reaches beyond social media into personal lives and corporations. People are caring more about feelings and developing the soft skills that just a few decades ago were pushed aside as unimportant. Things like conflict resolution, understanding your personality, and building strong teams have gained the traction they deserve. The era of relying solely on a leader to make the big decisions has become less and less a reality, replaced by properly harnessing and channeling the opinions of the masses. And with this comes the necessary emphasis on the roles that mental and emotional health play.

As with everything else we discussed so far, this idea of caring about our feelings and maintaining a healthy self-image can be taken in a positive direction or a negative direction. Knowing how you feel when around others and monitoring your interactions with them is healthy. Never moving from awareness to action is not healthy. It keeps you in the storm cloud and out of the light. Knowing yourself is a terrific first step, and I hope this book has helped awaken you to where you are in your relationships, as well as where you'd ideally like to be.

As egocentric as human nature tends to be, the amazing part of keeping firm boundaries is that it allows us to focus on other people. Instead of feeling pushed around or behind in our obligations, or running from one commitment to another, establishing boundary lines and holding firmly to our tug of war rope, frees up a wealth of energy, observations, time, and emotion to work for us and our benefit. In doing so, each of us is given opportunities to look around us and see where we can help or encourage someone else. Plus, with boundaries, we can maintain control, giving us the freedom to bask in the light of a balanced life.

Getting control of your life *does not* mean that you become cold, self-serving, or demanding of others. Frankly, it has less to do *about* others and more to do with our own mentality than you may think. Nothing in this book suggests that we should ever attempt to control others as a means of ending their control over us. Instead, the emphasis has been on our own changing as a human being—that by changing our thoughts and monitoring our feelings we are taking responsibility for our own lives. It has nothing to do with the choices that someone else may be making. This change has everything to do with us—what we will allow to influence us, and our personal behaviors.

So far in life, you may feel that you are simply coping with the stress and pressure you've been living under for so long. You may have begun to identify several defense strategies and points of denial in your life. If we want to move from merely *coping* to actually *thriving*, we will need to embrace the call of steady action.

That means, every day we must do something to make a change in our lives. We will need to be consistent and self-assured, no matter what our feelings are telling us. Once we move beyond coping with the loss of boundaries to actually managing our boundaries, we will enjoy a new level of freedom.

The work is not finished until we resolve our boundary issues. In resolving these, we are planting our feet firmly in the ground and determining that our foundational rights to self-control are more important than the temporary relief found in giving control away. We will stand resolutely and not back down. We will be kind about our boundaries, but they will stay in place despite repeated attempts by others to manipulate and move them.

If you want long-term peace in your life, begin today. Formulate your plan for returning your boundaries to their proper place. If you sense a lot of rigidity or defensiveness coming out of you after reading this book, you may want to scale back the changes and slow down your pace. If you are like me, whenever you learn something new that you feel is of value, you will try to implement the lessons all at once. But it may be that what you have learned is too much to implement, manage, and monitor all at once. Slow down. Take each issue one at a time. Focus on the most important one first. Remember, being busy or over committing is one form of giving control away to others.

Our actions follow our thoughts. If you are in a healthy place, your actions will show it. If things are getting a bit too much to handle, your actions will also show that.

~§~
Making life changes takes time. Be patient as you rebuild areas of your life that you believe need improvement.
~§~

Think of a little child playing with building blocks. Carefully they stack one on top of the other. If they haphazardly throw them together the blocks will tumble. If they take their time and use their mind to wisely choose each spot to place a block, then the structure won't tumble. If they build a firm foundation for the structure, then it will remain solid even when some of the upper blocks fall. This is what you are doing now. You're building a foundation. Make it strong. Make it lasting.

ABOUT THE AUTHOR

Sheena Monnin is the CEO of Custom Life Design, a consulting company that specializes in Leadership Development, Conflict Resolution, and Team Building for individuals and corporations.

Sheena's passion for human development led her to attain her Master's Degree in Psychology. She has also achieved a double-certification as an Enneagram Personality Expert.

Sheena is actively involved in Toastmasters International and has over ten years of public speaking experience. She is available for speaking engagements.

If you have questions or would like to talk about how Custom Life Design can help you or your company, please contact us:

Email: Sheena@customlifedesign.com

Website: www.customlifedesign.com.

www.ingramcontent.com/pod-product-compliance
Lightning Source LLC
Chambersburg PA
CBHW072012040426
42447CB00009B/1594